WESTLAND
LYSANDER

1936–46 (all marks)

First published in November 2014

A catalogue record for this book is available from the British Library.

ISBN 978 0 85733 395 7

Published by Haynes Publishing,
Sparkford, Yeovil,
Somerset BA22 7JJ, UK.
Tel: 01963 442030 Fax: 01963 440001
Int. tel: +44 1963 442030
Int. fax: +44 1963 440001
E-mail: sales@haynes.co.uk
Website: www.haynes.co.uk

Haynes North America Inc.,
861 Lawrence Drive, Newbury Park,
California 91320, USA.

Printed in the USA by Odcombe Press LP,
1299 Bridgestone Parkway, La Vergne,
TN 37086.

WESTLAND LYSANDER

1936–46 (all marks)

Owners' Workshop Manual

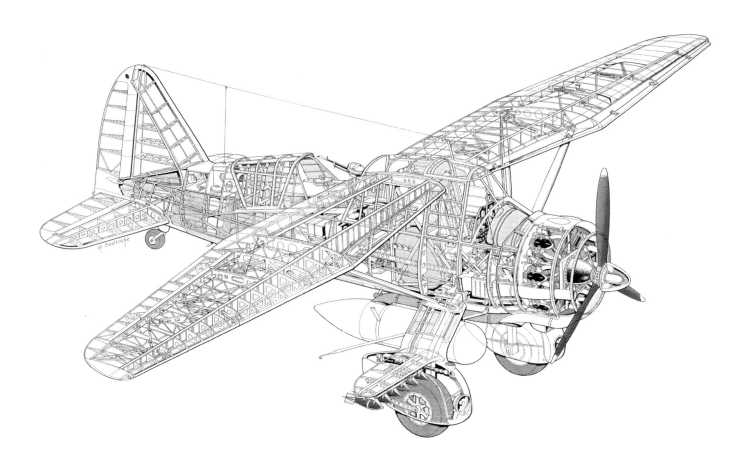

An insight into owning, flying and maintaining the RAF's
famous Second World War 'cloak-and-dagger' spy plane

Edward Wake-Walker

Contents

OPPOSITE Westland Lysander V9281 (G-BCWL) pictured over Yeovil in June 1993. *(PRM Aviation Collection)*

ABOVE The Shuttleworth Collection's Lysander (V9367) displays to the crowd at Old Warden airfield in 2002. *(PRM Aviation Collection)*

Introduction

'The clothes you're wearing, the room, the house, the city that you're in. Everything in it started out in the human imagination.'

Alan Moore, *Promethea*, volume 5

This may sound obvious, but it is important, in a book whose subject is an aeroplane, to remember that every machine is only the reflection of the people who created it, used it and looked after it. Their story is as important as the description of the nuts and bolts. Therefore, if the Westland Lysander – the 'Lizzie' – proved inadequate for the task for which it was originally conceived, it would be wrong to blame the machine or its inventors. After all, they produced an aircraft that, through a thoroughly innovative design, came closer than any other to fitting the awkward specification set out by the military. The aircraft and its pilots were forced to operate under a mistaken perception of modern warfare and became as much victims of the German *Blitzkrieg* and its air support in 1940 as the men of the British Expeditionary Force that they were deployed to assist.

And yet, even if the Lysander was not quite as instrumental in turning round the war for Britain as such icons as the Spitfire, the Hurricane, the Mosquito and the Lancaster bomber, there is still a deep residual affection for this stubby veteran of the Second World War. Even if it was too slow for the Messerschmitts in the Battle of France, it was a friendly presence in the sky for the beleaguered troops as they fought their way back to the beaches of Dunkirk. Then, when invasion threatened, the sight of Lysanders patrolling coastal waters of the UK must have lent encouragement to a nation permanently

BELOW A Lysander fuselage is welded in a jig at the Westland factory in 1937. *(AgustaWestland)*

on edge. It certainly gave heart to many downed pilots from the Battle of Britain who had the Lysander air-sea rescue pilots to thank for their deliverance from the waters of the North Sea and the English Channel.

It was an equally welcome sight for the desert armies in North Africa, both in the initial victories over Italian forces, then in the see-sawing battles with Rommel in 1941. And the throaty roar of its Bristol engine as the Lysanders passed overhead on their way to drop bombs on enemy positions would have quickened the hearts of Allied troops fighting in the jungles of Burma, albeit while they were mainly in retreat.

It is strange that the reason the Lysander is best remembered today is for a service it gave which was witnessed by virtually no one at the time. This, of course, was the special duties role of No 161 Squadron, providing a moonlit top-secret taxi service in and out of occupied France and Belgium for agents of the SOE and MI6. For these brave individuals the Lysanders and their pilots represented a lifeline that could deliver them from the threat of torture and death at the hands of Nazi interrogators. They were also the indispensable means of waging a clandestine war against their occupiers and,

ABOVE Lysander production underway at Yeovil. (*AgustaWestland*)

therefore, for those agents who survived the war, a joint function of man and machine that should be remembered forever.

BELOW Lysander Mk IIIA, V9289, of No 357 Squadron over Burma in 1945.
(*Andy Thomas collection*)

Chapter One

The Lysander story

The war in the air over the trenches of the Western Front in 1916 was still a strong influence on those who drew up the Air Ministry's specification for a new Army co-operation aircraft in 1935. Westland's of Yeovil, at the time comparative minnows among aircraft manufacturers, won the contract with its Lysander, the best solution to the awkward demand for speed and a short take-off and landing capability.

OPPOSITE Lysander V9281 overflies its birthplace at Yeovil in June 1993. Beneath her can be seen the Westland factory complex and airfield. *(PRM Aviation Collection)*

It is a day late in July 1916, and the first to dawn fine and clear over the Somme battleground for more than a week. Lieutenantt Leslie Horridge of No 7 Squadron of the Royal Flying Corps is airborne and heading towards a town some seven miles behind enemy lines. His task is to direct the artillery whose 5in guns are about to start pounding this strategic supply point with high-explosive shells. The role of his observer, seated just behind him, is to relay to the gunners via radio telegraphy where their shells are landing in relation to their chosen target.

It is a high-risk mission. Their slow but steady BE2 C reconnaissance aircraft has a maximum speed of 72mph and takes more than 45 minutes to climb to its service ceiling of 10,000ft. Its only defence is a 0.303in Lewis gun mounted in the observer's cockpit, coupled with the evasive skills of the pilot. Although the British and French forces have won a measure of supremacy in the air by the time of the Battle of the Somme, the German Fokker fighters present a major threat, with their forward-firing machine guns, synchronised so that the bullets pass through their spinning propeller blades.

For that reason, Horridge is accompanied by one of the RFC's own fighters, a DH2, but even before they reach the line the two aircraft get separated and Horridge is forced to cross over unescorted. As he approaches the

target, flying at about 5,000ft, a German LVG reconnaissance aircraft – similar in performance to his own – turns towards him. He shouts over his shoulder to his observer to be ready with the Lewis gun but cannot make himself heard. It is only when the German plane opens fire that the rearward-seated airman wheels round in alarm as bullets whistle past his ear.

The pilot of the LVG, conscious of his own plane's limitations as a means of aggressive combat, soon leaves the scene and Horridge and his observer, unscathed, prepare for their task over the target. The artillery shells are now landing on the town, and the circling BE2 C begins its signalled reports. Horridge has spotted four unidentified aircraft up ahead but they appear to show no interest in the British plane. Two of them remain in sight, keeping their distance, allowing Horridge and his observer to continue their task.

Then there is a tapping sound to the rear of the aircraft. Horridge thinks it might be a bit of his tail flapping in the wind, having been caught by some flak when he crossed the enemy's lines. He looks round to see a German Fokker diving down towards him, some 400yds away, its machine gun chattering as it gains on him. Horridge makes an evasive turn but the German pilot remains on his tail. The observer is on his feet swinging the Lewis gun through 180°, firing in five-bullet bursts, sometimes over the tail, sometimes over his pilot's head, as they fight to shake off their attacker.

Soon the British plane's gun falls silent. The drum of 47 rounds is spent and the observer cannot reach another magazine (such is the aircraft's ill-designed stowage configuration). By now the Fokker is within about 150ft and still firing. Horridge knows that it will be only moments before he or his observer, or both, are strafed by the bullets. But then the chattering stops and the German peels away from his prey. At once Horridge realises that his pursuer has also used up his belt of 150 rounds and is calling off the hunt. The three other aircraft he saw have also disappeared, their task as a decoy, he now deduces, no longer required. At this point, his own fighter escort reappears beside him and he can resume his artillery cooperation task in relative safety. He has time now to consider that had the Fokker pilot not opened fire so early in his attack he could have surprised him and his observer at much closer range, and would have had enough ammunition to be certain to finish them off.

The BE2 C featured in this account, along with another two-seater biplane, the RE 8, served as workhorses for the Royal Flying Corps in its army cooperation tasks during the First World War. The 'dug-in' nature of the conflict meant that aerial reconnaissance of enemy trenches, artillery positions and supply

LEFT LVG C.II German two-seat reconnaissance biplane. Note the Bergman machine gun in the rear gunner's turret. *(Bundesarchiv)*

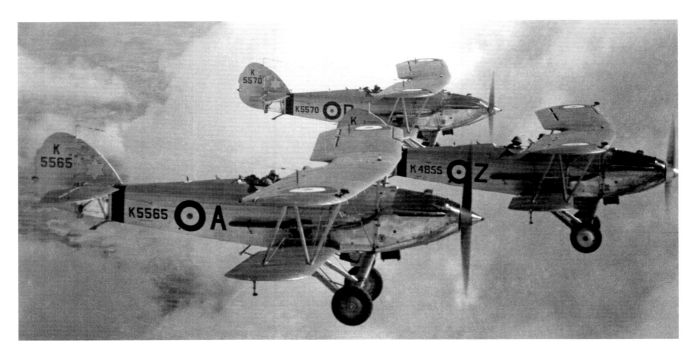

(Philip Jarrett)

lines became a vital part of the attritional process of identifying crucial targets and blasting them in the hope of weakening the enemy prior to an infantry assault.

That such indispensable instruments of war should emerge in little more than a decade after the Wright brothers' first flight in a powered heavier-than-air machine in December 1903, demonstrates how the dire necessities of trench warfare proved such a fertile mother of invention. In the 21-year interim between the two world wars warplane development naturally became less focused, as the requirements for any future conflict were less obvious. Fortunately this did not prevent some far-sighted projects going ahead, such as the Hawker Hurricane and the Supermarine Spitfire, both of which provided the RAF with fast monoplane interceptor fighters in time for the renewed hostilities with Germany in 1939.

But in the field of army support and reconnaissance, those officers responsible for procuring suitable aircraft found it difficult to think outside the box that had been defined by the course of the war through which they had just lived. There was awareness, with the development of the tank and other armoured vehicles, that battlefronts would be shifting more rapidly in future conflicts, but how army support aircraft should adapt to meet such conditions was probably a subject to which little time and

collaborative thought was afforded. The RAF, keen to prove its value as a new sovereign service, independent of its army roots, put much emphasis on the need to provide a force of bombers and fighters that could wage a war on an entirely different front from that of the army or navy. The bombers would attack enemy airfields and other strategic military and industrial targets and the fighters would protect the bomber force and defend the country against hostile bombing raids.

So, as with so many divisions of labour where areas of interest overlap, the question of which men and machines were most suitable for army air support did not receive an entirely satisfactory answer. If the RAF were now to supply the pilots and the aircraft, how could the army be sure – in the field of artillery guidance, for instance – that the airmen were sufficiently versed in the dark arts of accurate shelling? Equally, would the aircraft be suitably designed and equipped for the very specific requirements of front-line troops? The days of fixed battle lines and reasonably adjacent airfields were quite possibly over. There was little chance that the Bristol Fighter, the Armstrong-Whitworth Atlas or the Hawker Audax – the current RAF aircraft most suited to army cooperation – would be close enough to hand, requiring, as they did, airfields of considerable size to take off and land.

One potential solution to providing on-the-spot aerial observation and communication between troops on the front line was the autogyro that was being developed by the Spanish engineer Juan de la Cierva. By March 1935 he had perfected a rotary-wing machine which could be kept under control at very slow speeds, could land practically from the vertical and that needed only a short length in which to become airborne. The Air Ministry had trialled some of his earlier models with some enthusiasm and, had not more pressing requirements at the outbreak of war and the death of la Cierva in an air crash in 1936 intervened, something with attributes close to the earliest helicopters might well have played a part in the army's struggle against Hitler. Instead, the British generals were to make do with an aircraft of much more conventional

appearance and operation: the Westland Lysander.

In February 1935 the Air Ministry had issued a specification for an aircraft to replace the Hawker Hector and Audax. With a maximum speed of 187mph, these army cooperation biplanes would now be easy prey for the modern fighters Germany was producing, such as the 350mph Me 109. The Ministry's long list of requirements was probably an attempt to incorporate what was known to have worked in the last war and what might be needed in the next, if, and when, it came. The stipulations for a two-seat aircraft with a good view in every conceivable direction, two forward-firing Browning guns, a rear Lewis gun in a rotating turret, provision for a camera, wireless set, bomb and other load-dropping facility, together with a message pick-up hook, all harked

LEFT A flight of the RAF's experimental C30 Cierva autogyros.
(Philip Jarrett)

LEFT AND CENTRE The Westland Pterodactyl design with its short take-off and landing capability helped the company to be included in the bid for a new army cooperation aircraft in 1935. *(AgustaWestland)*

back to how aircraft had been used over the trenches.

There were signs that some of the changing patterns of warfare were being taken into account, however. A self-starting, simple-to-maintain 890hp engine was specified, capable of achieving a speed of 245mph at 5,000ft and with an endurance of 3½ hours. More significant still was a requirement for take-off and landing to be achieved within 350yd of a 50ft obstacle and for the landing run to be no more than 150yd. Here was a signal that the new design should not have to depend upon established airfields, rather that it should operate as close as possible to a shifting battlefront by an ability to use shorter and more rudimentary runways.

Of the manufacturing companies who submitted designs against this specification, only two were asked to build prototypes. One was the Bristol Aeroplane Company, who had proposed a low-winged monoplane known as the Type 148. The other was Somerset-based Westland, who had not originally been invited to tender but who successfully argued their case with the Ministry to be included. This was based partly, at least, on their experience with the Pterodactyl series of designs, an ungainly looking tailless, high-winged flying machine in which the RAF had shown some interest but had ultimately discarded. One aspect that had attracted them originally was its short take-off and landing capability.

Westland was a firm whose roots lay in providing industrial support to agriculture. James Bazeley Petter was a farming engineer and iron founder who in 1896 had established a business in Yeovil known as J.B. Petter and

LEFT The workshop of J.B. Petter and Sons of Yeovil at the end of the 19th century when the family firm manufactured petrol and diesel engines for agricultural and light industrial purposes. *(AgustaWestland)*

Sons. The sons in question were identical twins Ernest and Percival. Their engineering flair had allowed the family firm to develop stationary petrol and diesel engines that became much in demand as a power source for both agricultural and light industrial machinery throughout the country. Their Nautilus Works in the middle of Yeovil had its own foundry and steel-working facilities, and by the outbreak of the First World War was producing 1,500 engines every year.

By 1915 the British government had begun to realise that its established armament factories would not be adequate to supply the insatiable demands of the war on the Western Front and an urgent appeal went out to manufacturers across the country to turn their facilities over to the war effort. The Petter twins (now in charge of the family company) were quick to respond, sending telegrams to the War Office and the Admiralty, offering to place their entire facilities and workforce at the government's disposal. While the War Office showed no interest, the Admiralty responded immediately and a meeting in London was soon arranged. The navy was looking for somewhere to build patrol seaplanes, and Yeovil, famous for the sewing skills of those working in its local glove-making industry, combined with the engineering knowhow of J.B. Petter and Sons, was potentially ideal for the manufacture of such fabric-clad aircraft.

Very quickly a division of the Petter business was established under the name of Westland Aircraft Works, and work began on the first order from the navy for 12 Short Type 184 seaplanes. Orders for more seaplanes soon followed, together with another for Sopwith 1½ Strutters, and by 1916 a dedicated Westland aircraft factory and airfield was under construction.

By the time of the Air Ministry's 1935 specification for a new army cooperation aircraft, Westland had become firmly established as a designer and supplier to the military. Its 122kt Wapiti, first built in 1927, was the mainstay of

LEFT Where old and new technologies meet: biplane wings are transported at Westland during the company's earliest years of aircraft construction. *(AgustaWestland)*

BELOW Vickers Vimy bomber wings under construction at Westland's factory in 1919. *(AgustaWestland)*

RIGHT The Westland Wapiti: this successful biplane helped to put Westland's name on the map, especially after an adapted version of the design was used in the first flight over Mount Everest in 1933. *(AgustaWestland)*

ABOVE Ten six-seat Westland Wessex airliners were built in 1929–30. This is OO-AGE that was acquired by Belgian national airline Sabena in August 1930. Sir Alan Cobham bought the aircraft in 1935 for operation between England and the Channel Islands. It ditched in the English Channel on 3 July 1935 after suffering engine failure on a flight from Guernsey. The pilot and two passengers died, but one was rescued. *(AgustaWestland)*

RIGHT W.E.W. (Teddy) Petter, Westland's technical director and the man who designed the Lysander. *(AgustaWestland)*

the RAF's general-purpose fleet between the wars. In all 558 Wapitis were built at Westland, providing enough work at the factory to stave off the worst effects of the Depression, which sent so many contemporary businesses to the wall. It was a modified version of the Wapiti, the Westland-Houston PV-3, which was the first aircraft to fly over the 29,000ft summit of Mount Everest in 1933, a much-publicised feat across the globe that added considerably to the kudos of the company.

In 1935 the eyebrows – and in some cases the hackles – of senior Westland staff were raised with the appointment of W.E.W. (Teddy) Petter as technical director of the company. He was the Marlborough College and Cambridge-educated son of Ernest Petter who had joined the company in 1929 as a trainee, having graduated with a first-class degree in mechanical sciences, but who was still only 27 years old at his appointment. Either because they thought that other, more experienced individuals were worthier of the post, or simply because they disliked his somewhat aloof demeanour, a number of valuable people resigned from the company. Even the Air Ministry's confidence in Westland was threatened by the appointment – which explains, perhaps, why they were left off the original list of those invited to tender for the new army cooperation aircraft.

It was fortunate for Teddy Petter and the company that two key individuals decided to remain on board. One was Arthur Davenport, the seasoned chief designer, who had himself been a strong candidate for the technical director post. The other was Harald Penrose, Westland's highly competent chief test pilot. Between them, these three men consulted widely among the pilots and maintenance crews of the army cooperation squadrons before they committed themselves to the drawing board. They studied the squadrons' operational methods and received often conflicting opinions on the type of new aircraft that was required.

For all his youth and poor inter-personal skills, Teddy Petter's resulting design solution comprised a number of innovations which would mark him down as an engineer of rare originality and would see him go on to design the famous post-war jet-engined English Electric Canberra and provide much of the conceptual thought which led to the same company's supersonic Lightning.

Westland's P8 (as the prototype was called), powered by an 840hp Bristol Mercury IX air-cooled radial engine, emerged from the factory shed in June 1936 with some highly distinctive features. To afford the best possible all-round visibility from the cockpit, the high wing was tapered on the inboard leading edge, giving the aircraft a gull-wing appearance, especially when viewed from above or below. A single aluminium-alloy extrusion, bent into a wishbone shape, formed the legs for the undercarriage, keeping the forward fuselage well clear of any rough ground and providing tremendous resilience in a hard landing.

Most remarkable of all were the retracting slats along the full length of the wings' leading edges. These were linked to slotted trailing-edge flaps, both of which would deploy automatically to produce maximum lift as the pilot slowed for landing, allowing the aircraft to touch down at the lowest possible speed. Their ability to retract

LEFT Westland's chief designer, Arthur Davenport. *(AgustaWestland)*

BELOW Arthur Davenport (seated) with members of his team. *(AgustaWestland)*

LEFT Westland's chief test pilot and the first man to fly the Lysander, Harald Penrose. *(AgustaWestland)*

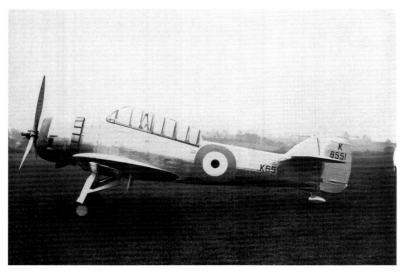

ABOVE The Bristol 148, the only design to come off the drawing board to compete with Westland's P8 as a solution to the RAF's 1935 specification for a new army cooperation design. *(Philip Jarrett)*

the challenging minimum take-off and landing stipulation. However, the Bristol's cause cannot have been helped by a landing accident during the Air Ministry's comparative trials, and the decision to go with the Westland design was also swayed by its superior visibility due to the shape and position of the wings and its fixed and sturdy undercarriage (as opposed to the Bristol's retractable forward wheels). Interestingly, the Ministry chose to overlook the fact that the Westland P8 fell short by some 15% of their specified maximum speed of 245mph while the Bristol 148 could achieve 290mph. They might well have regretted this compromise during the torrid summer of 1940 over the fields of northern France.

gave the aircraft much greater speed through the air than any of its contemporary short take-off and landing designs that used fixed leading-edge slots, which were inevitably slowed by the drag of the device.

How did this unusual aircraft compare with its low-winged rival, the Bristol 148? Both met

But there were other problems for the Westland team to overcome before their design was finally accepted by the RAF. On the prototype's maiden flight from the Wiltshire RAF base at Boscombe Down, on 15 June 1936, test pilot Harald Penrose discovered problems with the aircraft's inherent longitudinal stability

RIGHT AND OPPOSITE The 1936 Lysander prototype (K6127) is put through her paces. *(RAF Museum)*

ABOVE King Edward VIII ascends a ladder for a closer look at the prototype Lysander on an official visit to the Aeroplane & Armament Experimental Establishment (A&AEE) at Martlesham Heath, Suffolk, in 1936 during his brief reign. *(RAF Museum)*

BELOW Hawker Hectors were built under licence by Westland's. Here, airframes are seen in the erecting shop during 1937. *(AgustaWestland)*

and, more worryingly, when he brought her in to land the effect of the automatic slots and flaps meant that the only way to level out for touchdown was to put on extra engine power. Although the instability was fairly easily cured by increasing the tailplane area, the only way to achieve a means of levelling out on landing was to make the incidence of the tailplane adjustable by a manual cockpit control wheel.

Penrose was not in favour of this solution. He was particularly concerned about when a pilot needed to climb quickly away from an aborted landing. With the tailplane still in its landing position, the engine fully open and the stick pushed hard forward, the aircraft reared up steeply, 'heading uncontrollably for a stall', as he described it in his memoir *Adventure with Fate*.

'The only safe method,' he concluded, 'was to increase power just sufficiently to maintain speed with slots fully open, meanwhile tugging away with the left hand at the many turns necessary to reset the tailplane incidence to neutral. That was bound to cause some fatal accidents.'

In spite of Penrose's protestations that the design was flawed, Teddy Petter was reluctant to make further changes as it would disrupt the company's lucrative production programme.

Instead he handed the decision on the system's safety to the Air Ministry's testing establishment at Martlesham Heath and, to Penrose's dismay, the RAF pilots there accepted the system for operational use.

By the time the second prototype was built, in December 1936, other modifications had been incorporated into the design, including steps built into the spats and fuselage to aid the pilot's ascent into the cockpit, and machine guns mounted both in the rear cockpit and in the wheel spats. The time was now ripe to give this brave new warplane a suitably heroic type-name, and so she became the Westland Lysander – named after the great Spartan general forever linked, in the song *The British Grenadiers*, with Hector, another ferocious adversary of the ancient Greeks. (The Hawker Hector was the biplane predecessor of the Lysander in army cooperation and subcontracted to Westland for production in the late 1930s.)

The second prototype gave the RAF an opportunity to test the Lysander in hot and tropical climates after it was shipped out to India, then flown back to Britain, taking in more trials in the Middle East en route. Soon after its

ABOVE **The second Lysander prototype (K6128), the first to be fitted with machine guns in the wheel spats and the rear cockpit. This aircraft was shipped out to India for hot-weather trials and flown back to the UK via the Middle East. During a test flight back in the UK it met with near calamity when the wing fabric tore away in a rapid dive.** *(Shuttleworth Collection)*

BELOW **K6128 on trials in India.** *(PRM Aviation Collection)*

RIGHT The damaged wing of K6128 after the experimental, lighter-weight fabric peeled away as the aircraft dived. Squadron Leader R.W.P. Collings was awarded the Air Force Cross for his skill in saving himself and the aircraft. *(The National Archives)*

BELOW LEFT AND RIGHT In a similar incident to the one affecting the second prototype in 1937, the fabric has been stripped from the wing of this target-towing Lysander Mk IIIA (W6-1, V9295) after it had been put into a 250kt dive by its Royal Navy pilot above RNAS Worthy Down, Hampshire, in January 1944. *(Shuttleworth Collection)*

return, what at first appeared to be a very serious setback in the aircraft's acceptability occurred in the skies above Suffolk. Squadron Leader R.W.P. Collings was carrying out advanced handling trials and put the plane into a rapid dive up to the limit of its tolerance. Suddenly the pilot noticed that the fabric on the top surface of the wings was flapping wildly and, as he fought to recover the plane, much of it tore away completely. Rather than baling out, the pilot chose to attempt to bring the plane down and, because the flaps still worked and the slats provided strong suction

over the wing's metal leading edge, accomplished a terrifyingly fast landing back at the Martlesham aerodrome. He was awarded the Air Force Cross for his skill and courage. Back at Westland there was an immediate realisation that their attempt to save weight in the second prototype, by using glider fabric rather than the Irish linen used in the first, was a serious misjudgement. By now, though, the Air Ministry's order for 169 airframes was in full production swing and in June 1938 the first operational Lysander was delivered to the RAF's No 16 Squadron.

LEFT Lysanders under construction at the Westland factory. *(AgustaWestland)*

BELOW LEFT The first production Lysander (Mk I, L4673) ready for delivery from the Westland factory. *(RAF Museum)*

BELOW Lysander Mk Is of No 16 Squadron, the first RAF squadron to operate the aircraft in May 1938. *(RAF Museum)*

LEFT A line of Mk II Lysanders at Yeovil ready for delivery to the RAF. N1203 in the foreground was allocated to the RAF's Parachute Practice Flight at Ringway, Manchester, and later went missing on what is believed to have been an early Special Duties operation on 18 August 1940. *(AgustaWestland)*

RIGHT A pre-war Lysander in French livery; France had ordered a single Lysander for their own evaluation in 1936. The order was never delivered, however, after a French test pilot misread the cambered runway at Westland's airstrip and badly damaged the Lysander he was bringing in to land. *(AgustaWestland)*

A Lysander Mk I (Y517) flown by No 1 Army Cooperation Squadron, Royal Egyptian Air Force, photographed in 1941. Westland supplied a total of 19 Lysanders to Egypt in 1938. *(AgustaWestland)*

ABOVE Not German, but Finnish: the Finns (who used the swastika motif on their aircraft between 1918 and 1945) were customers of Westland in 1939 when they ordered 12 Lysanders to repel a Russian invasion in November of that year. LY-118 (of unit 2Le.Lv.16) is a Mk I and is pictured in August 1942. *(PRM Aviation Collection)*

BELOW Don't shoot at me! Royal Canadian Air Force Lysander Mk III (2307) was used for target-towing with No 8 Bombing & Gunnery School, Lethbridge, Alberta, circa 1942. She wears high visibility black and yellow-striped markings. Westland's supplied 104 British-built Lysanders to Canada, augmenting 225 that were licence-built by National Steel Car at Malton, Ontario. *(RAF Museum)*

Chapter Two

Lysander at war

Suffering huge losses at the hands of the Luftwaffe during the Battle of France in 1940, the RAF's Lysander squadrons retreated to home airfields and adopted defensive and air-sea rescue roles. Further afield, where enemy fighter power was less intense, Lysanders provided more effective assistance to British troops in Egypt, Libya, Madagascar and Burma.

OPPOSITE Maintenance under a hot sun for the Lysanders of No 208 Squadron. Note the desert camouflage scheme, the toned-down fuselage markings, and absence of serial numbers and fin flashes. *(RAF Museum)*

ABOVE Three Lysanders of No 16 Squadron in Munich Crisis markings fly in formation over Salisbury Cathedral, close to their base at Old Sarum. The squadron was the first to receive Lysanders, although it continued to operate its old Hawker Audaxes until October 1938. By the time of the Munich Crisis in late October the squadron was fully operational on Lysanders. *(RAF Museum)*

As the threat of war with Germany first loomed during the Munich Crisis through the autumn of 1938, then receded, then returned in the spring of 1939 after Hitler had marched into Prague, Lysander numbers had grown rapidly across the country. No 16 Squadron, the first to receive Westland Lysanders in the summer of 1938, was stationed at Old Sarum, just north of Salisbury, the home also of the RAF's School of Army Cooperation. Here, as the Mk I version rolled off the Yeovil production line, instructors at the school and pilots of the squadron undertook training at the same airfield on this intriguing new aeroplane, soon to be affectionately nicknamed the 'Lizzie'. By the outbreak of war seven Lysander squadrons had been formed, most of which began to operate the Mk II version of the aircraft, which used a more powerful 905hp Bristol Perseus engine.

The novelty of the Lysander's slow-flying prowess led a few RAF pilots into a false sense of security. Three lives were lost on one fateful day in April 1939, when, first, a No 2 Squadron pilot, demonstrating the plane's capabilities at Hawkinge in Kent, stalled his aircraft after going into a steep climb with apparently insufficient power. Too near the ground to recover from the stall, he crashed, killing himself and his crewman. Meanwhile, another Lysander had just taken off from Denham airfield in Buckinghamshire when it, too, was made to climb too steeply, with the same fatal result for its lone pilot. Urgently, the Air Ministry issued an order that the Lysander should never be made to climb steeply at an altitude of less than 600ft or to climb at all when travelling at under 50mph. Sadly this did not prevent another slow and low-flying fatal accident the following month, this time at the RAF Empire Air Day

ABOVE AND RIGHT Pilots and ground crew of No 2 Squadron at Hawkinge in Kent, among the first to fly a Lysander, examine their newly delivered aircraft (Mk I, L4705) in 1938. The squadron was commanded by Squadron Leader A.J.W. Geddes who, like many army cooperation squadron commanders of the day, had been seconded to the RAF from the Royal Artillery.
(AgustaWestland/Andy Thomas collection)

display at Ringway, Manchester, where it was a turning manoeuvre at 200ft that induced a stall.

In spite of these setbacks, by the time of Hitler's invasion of Poland on 1 September 1939, and the subsequent British declaration of war with Germany two days later, there were enough Lysanders built and pilots trained to equip six army cooperation squadrons, posted across the Channel to assist the British Expeditionary Force. The deployment of the BEF, consisting in its early days of some 158,000 troops, was a show of strength and readiness, in alliance with the French, to assist Poland in her defence against the German invasion. Apart from an inconsequential and short-lived incursion by the French into the German Saar region of the Rhine valley, the Allies resolved in the end to take up a defensive position, the French behind the fortified Maginot line and the British along the Franco-Belgian

border. The six Lysander squadrons (Nos 2, 4, 13, 26, 225 and 614) were divided into two wings, the 51st near the coast and the 50th about 50 miles inland.

Had the Allies made a more decisive blow against Germany's western defences while her attention was focused on the fight with Poland, there might have been a much speedier outcome to the war. As it was, with French and British divisions outnumbering the Germans' by about four to one, both sides dug in and waited. Through the winter months of the 'Phoney War', as it became known, there was very little for the army cooperation pilots to do. Both adversaries were careful not to be seen infringing the neutrality of the buffer states of the Netherlands, Belgium or Luxembourg, and therefore the Lysander crews spent most of their time aloft, practising evasive action with the aid of Gladiator biplane fighters.

RIGHT The severe winter of 1939–40 made for very uncomfortable living conditions for British servicemen in northern France. This Lysander Mk II (L4767, 'OO-F') of No 13 Squadron has suffered a sudden loss of tyre pressure amidst the wintry surroundings of its base at Mons-en-Chausée in February 1940. *(Andy Thomas collection)*

Three Lysanders were lost in this period, but not through enemy action. Insufficient operational training for young pilots who joined their squadrons in France straight from Flying Training Schools was the real cause of these accidents, all of which happened during manoeuvres close to the ground. Another adversary at the time was the very severe winter of 1939/40, with heavy snow forcing Nos 2 and 4 Squadrons to move from their airfield with tented accommodation to billets a few miles further from the Belgian border.

RIGHT Sqn Ldr A.J.W. Geddes, CO of No 2 Squadron in France in 1940. *(Copyright unknown)*

When news arrived on 10 May 1940 that all Germany's inhibitions had been cast aside in a ruthless and simultaneous advance into neutral Holland, Belgium and Luxembourg, the same two squadrons accompanied the BEF eastwards into Belgium to a position along the River Dyle. The Allies' plan to weaken Hitler's military by blockading her western front had patently failed. Rather, with a show of great strength and speed, German armoured divisions roared through the dense forests of the Ardennes, found inadequate resistance from the French Ninth Army and, within five days of the offensive, were spreading out across the French countryside west of Sedan.

The course of the *Blitzkrieg* now turned west and then north towards the Channel coast, thrusting past Cambrai and Arras and along the Somme, making a mockery of the stasis of the war that had been fought over that landscape 25 years earlier. The effect of this electrifying advance was to isolate the northern half of the Belgian, French and British armies and give them little alternative other than to retreat ever further towards the northern French coast. The first withdrawal by the BEF began on 16 May, moving westward from their original position along the River Dyle to another river, the Scheldt.

The withdrawal would only be possible if the bridges over the Scheldt were not already in enemy hands. Therefore, among the several reconnaissance missions being asked of the Lysander crews, it fell to the commander of No 2 Squadron, Wing Commander Andrew Geddes, to find out whether the river was still safe to cross. With fighter aircraft mainly occupied in defending troops on the ground from German air attacks, protection was seldom provided for reconnaissance flights. So instead of sending one of his young Lysander pilots on this particularly risky solo mission, Wing Commander Geddes chose to go himself.

As he neared the bridges, he and his gunner, LAC Clarke, realised they had company. Two formations of Ju87 Stuka dive-bombers were circling at about 5,000ft above a bridge over the river. There were ten aircraft making up each section. It was obvious to Geddes that they were preparing to blow the bridge to pieces. In a later account of his experience, Geddes wrote:

'We felt rather exposed. Then Clarke, a brave chap who was killed in Sicily in 1943 as a Pilot Officer, said to me; "that's not very fair, sir, I think we should teach the buggers a lesson". I had only two options; surprise and offensive action. My Lysander KO-T was in splendid condition for a scrap. We took the initiative before the Germans could either bomb the bridge or shoot us down. Evidently their leader had mistaken us for a German Henschel Hs126 army co-op aircraft which looks somewhat like a "Lizzie"; a similar parasol wing, radial engine and fixed undercarriage.'

Taking full advantage of the mistaken identity, Geddes slowly attached himself to the back of the second formation. 'Then', his account continues, 'the first Stuka went down to bomb and others followed. I knew that the air gunner would not see us while his pilot went down in a steep dive. When the last Stuka pulled up I did the same and gave him a long burst. The bullets of the Vickers in the wheel spats hit him and I saw bits and pieces coming off. To my surprise, however, it did not catch fire and seemed to stagger on without any apparent

ABOVE The opposition 1: a Messerschmitt Bf109E of I./ Jagdgeschwader 27 (JG27) escorts a Junkers Ju87B Stuka of II./ Sturzkampfgeschwader 2 (StG2). Both units saw extensive action during the Battle of France in May–June 1940 with JG27 scoring heavily against Allied aircraft. *(Bundesarchiv)*

LEFT The opposition 2: Lysander look-alike: during the Battle of France British gunners sometimes confused the Lysander for the German Henschel Hs126, which also shared a similar parasol-wing design. *(Bundesarchiv)*

WESTLAND "LYSANDER" ON ACTIVE SERVICE

WESTLAND

WESTLAND AIRCRAFT LIMITED · YEOVIL · ENGLAND

his dive brakes and appeared to stop dead in the air straight ahead of me. I was forced to overshoot him and then all he needed to do was apply power, pull up his nose and have a go at me with his machine guns.'

To Geddes' relief the Stuka's bullets passed between the wing struts and the cockpit window on the starboard side. By now Clarke's gun was back in order and his pilot was able to manoeuvre the Lysander so that the Stuka was back in his crewman's sights. A long burst from the Lewis gun delivered a mortal blow. The aircraft began to smoke, the pilot baled out and Geddes saw the Stuka crash into a forest.

'I made sure I got away,' he wrote, 'sometimes following the roads to Wevelghem with my undercarriage between the trees, to stay as low as I possibly could. I remember that on several occasions we flew under power cables. Clarke said, "Sir, I prefer to look backwards, it saves me from seeing these lines coming closer."'

The 'kill' was confirmed when, after Geddes landed safely back at base, one of his officers raced in a car to the reported crash site at Kluisbergen, near Oudenaarde. He returned with a piece of the Stuka, although the trophy was soon lost when the squadron fled towards the coast to avoid capture by German tanks a few days later.

No 2 Squadron recorded another remarkable success when, three days after, Flying Officer Tony Doidge, the same man who had retrieved the Stuka souvenir for his CO, was in action in Lysander KO-U against a Henschel 126 over the French town of Merville. While he managed to shoot down the German army cooperation aircraft, his gunner accounted for a Stuka in the same mission. Tragically, barely a week later on 1 June, Tony Doidge and his gunner, Sergeant Ian

damage. This was rather frustrating for now I had lost the element of surprise.'

As he closed in he guessed that he must have hit the gunner for the man had disappeared below the line of the fuselage and his gun barrel was vertical. The formation had now broken up in panic, but it was not long before Geddes' Lysander came under attack from the leading Stukas.

'I went down to ground level in defensive circles. At times my undercarriage brushed through the tree tops and then Clarke shouted through the tube that he had a stoppage and could I please hang around a bit until he cleared it. I could beat the Stukas by making flat turns without spinning due to the large automatic flaps and slats. However it was obvious that one Stuka pilot was a professional for he almost caught me with a cunning trick.

'When I got on his tail he clapped open

Michelmore, were lost when their Lysander was shot down by a German fighter over the Channel near La Panne, close to the Dunkirk beaches.

One other rare victory for the Lysander during this torrid period came when the aircraft of No 4 Squadron were being withdrawn from their base at Ronchin back to Boulogne on 18 May. Soon after take-off they were set upon by six Messerschmitt Bf 110s. A running fight ensued, with the Lysander pilots relying heavily on their low speed at very low altitude to force the large German aircraft to overshoot. Most of the squadron got away and there was even a claim from one of the crew members that he had shot down one of the enemy fighters. Two Lysanders never made it, however. Both were shot down and their crews killed. One of the pilots, Pilot Officer Plumb, had only been with the squadron a week.

By 22 May all but a single flight of the six Lysander squadrons originally sent to France had withdrawn to bases in Britain along the Channel coast. A handful of aircraft and crews from No 4 Squadron stayed in France a little longer until the surviving remnants made a bedraggled exit to Kent two days later. The task of providing reconnaissance for the BEF as it withdrew towards Dunkirk was practically impossible. The *Luftwaffe* had control of the skies, and any RAF fighter cover was being used to protect troops on the ground as they fought their rearguard action. The result was very heavy losses for Lysander crews, whether they were tasked from the English or the French side of the Channel, with no meaningful information getting through to the army commanders. Reconnaissance missions

were occasionally interspersed with equally futile bombing tasks, the Lizzie's 20lb bombs proving less than a pinprick against the German panzers and artillery. On at least two occasions, bombs which failed to release over the enemy fell from returning Lysanders as they landed back at base and detonated, destroying the aircraft.

In the days immediately leading up to the evacuation at Dunkirk, a fierce battle was fought by British and French troops in the defence of Calais. It was a fairly hopeless task, but Lysanders and Hectors from No 613 Squadron were ordered to dive-bomb the German positions surrounding the town on 26 May. The following day Lysander and Hector flights again crossed the Channel, this time to drop vital supplies to the besieged troops. It turned out to be a worthless mission as, unbeknown to the pilots, the Allied forces in Calais had already surrendered. Of the 16 aircraft and crews that took part in these sorties over Calais, 14 failed to return. Even an attempt by Lysander pilots to plot the German forward positions on special

ABOVE The opposition 3: *Oberleutnant* **Theodor Rossiwall (right), commander of 5./ Zerstörergeschwader 26 (ZG26), talks through a kill during the Battle of France with** *Major* **Johann Schalk (centre). Behind them is one of the squadron's Messerschmitt Bf 110 heavy fighters (note the four kills on the tail fin). On 19 May ZG26 claimed the destruction in combat of 19 Allied aircraft, with 9 more the next day. It would have been a pretty uneven match between a Lysander and the heavily armed Bf 110.** *(Bundesarchiv)*

LEFT British troops surrender to German forces after the fall of Calais in June 1940. *(Bundesarchiv)*

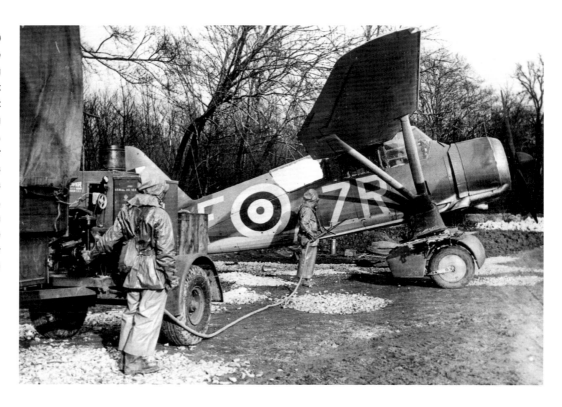

RIGHT During 1940 Lysanders were engaged in developing ground support techniques that included the spraying of poison gas, although it was never actually used. This is No 613 Squadron's Lysander Mk III, 'ZR-F', being cleaned after a gas-spraying exercise in late 1940. *(Andy Thomas collection)*

BELOW A survivor's eye-view of an overflying Lysander on an air-sea rescue mission. Note the box-shaped dinghy packs carried beneath the stub wings and smoke bombs for marking purposes under the rear fuselage. This particular aircraft is a Mk III that served with A Flight, No 277 Squadron. *(RAF Museum)*

maps and drop them to the troops gathered on the beaches of Dunkirk ran into difficulties. They found themselves being fired on by their own side as, once again, the Lysanders were mistaken for their German Henschel lookalikes.

Adding up the losses sustained by the Lysander squadrons during the failed Battle of France must have been a grim task. Eighty-eight of the aircraft had been shot down in air combat and a further 30 had been destroyed on the ground. That meant that nearly 70% of the 174-strong force of Lysanders used in the campaign had been lost and, more important still, 120 crew members were killed, with one squadron (No 4) also suffering a 60% casualty rate among its ground crew. The only conclusion to reach was that army air reconnaissance was no longer a task for slow aircraft with no fighter protection. Whatever the short take-off and landing qualities of the Lysander, a fast-moving battlefront was no place for such an aircraft. Very soon two newly developed single-seaters, the 360mph P-40 Tomahawk and the Auster, would take over its reconnaissance duties and the Lysander would be transferred to less offensive roles.

It took a little while for the lessons of the *Blitzkrieg* to work through the system,

LEFT Lost and found: a Lysander and RAF High Speed Launch demonstrate their search and rescue capabilities in an exercise at sea. However, this photograph may not be all that it seems because it is reputed to be an early attempt at a composite photograph for an RAF recruiting poster. *(RAF Museum)*

however, and in the period immediately following Dunkirk production of the Lysander continued apace at Yeovil, with plans even for a second factory to be established at Doncaster. Army cooperation squadrons began to receive Mk III replacements for the Lysanders lost over France, some with considerable dismay among the pilots, knowing as they did how unsuited the aircraft were for the part they were required to play. As the smoke cleared and the full realisation of the threat of a German invasion dawned, the new Ministry of Aircraft Production turned its attention towards the defence of the country. They stopped Lysander construction at the Doncaster factory after only 17 had come off the line, and turned their attention instead to producing new fighters and bombers.

Meanwhile, there was still a deadly serious task to be fulfilled by every able aircraft at the RAF's disposal in defending the British shores, and this included the Lysander squadrons. For much of the summer of 1940 they were sent on patrols over the Channel, spotting drifting mines and, in particular, looking out for any build-up of German troops and invasion barges in the occupied ports of Holland, Belgium and France. A vital search and rescue role was also assigned to Lysander pilots, looking for RAF crews who had been shot down over the sea. Their task was to spot the survivors in the water, drop an inflatable dinghy, mark their position with a smoke canister and call in a Walrus flying boat to pick them up. As the Battle of Britain raged Lysanders proved their worth in this role again and again, to the extent that in October 1941 four new squadrons (275–278) were established, dedicated to air-sea rescue. The crew of one Halifax bomber from No 35 Squadron, which had ditched in the sea 50 miles south of Portsmouth in December 1941, had a Lysander to thank for their lives. The pilot, having located the bomber crew in their emergency dinghy, then risked running out of fuel while he circled overhead for 90 minutes until a surface rescue vessel was able to reach them.

The Lysander continued in its air-sea rescue role throughout 1941 and 1942 and at the same time was also used by Fighter Command to tow targets at the end of a half-mile line for trainee gunners to practise air-to-air combat. It can only be called an unglamorous, if worthy, final service for an aircraft originally intended for front-line action assisting the British army to overcome German forces on the Continent.

Further afield

Ever since the second prototype Lysander was taken for trials in India and the Middle East in 1936, it was clear that the RAF believed it would have a role to play in other continents as well as Europe. By the time Italy joined the war on 10 June 1940 there were two RAF squadrons – No 6, based in Palestine, and No 208, based in Egypt – which were operating Lysanders in an army cooperation role. Italy had a total of 400,000 troops in Africa at this time, the British about 80,000. In spite of the imbalance in numbers and an aggressive move by the Italians in November 1940 to increase their territorial possessions into Egypt and the Sudan, they found more than a match in the three generals Wavell, Platt and Cunningham and their desert armies. By 18 May 1941, Wavell had won the surrender of the Italians in Libya, Platt had turned their troops out of the

Sudan and forced them back into Eritrea and Abyssinia, while Cunningham – approaching from Kenya in the south – had ensured a total capitulation as the two British armies met at Amba Alagi.

Wavell's success in the north was certainly aided by Lysander support, although, just as over France, enemy aircraft in the shape of Italian Fiat fighters were able to cramp their style considerably, especially as RAF fighter support was not always available. No 208 Squadron, which suffered the majority of Lysander losses, was involved in a major air battle on 20 November 1940 over Sidi Barrani. While a Lysander and a Blenheim carried out reconnaissance of enemy positions around the Egyptian coastal settlement, their escort – consisting of nine Hurricanes and six Gladiators – fought off Italian fighters for half an hour as the essential photographs were successfully gathered.

ABOVE The Pyramids of Giza form the backdrop to a trio of Lysander Mk Is of No 208 Squadron. *(RAF Museum)*

BELOW A No 208 Squadron Lysander (L4712) makes a supply drop over the Egyptian desert near Heliopolis. *(RAF Museum)*

BELOW No 208 Squadron (L4723) practises message collection in the desert near Heliopolis in 1939. *(RAF Museum)*

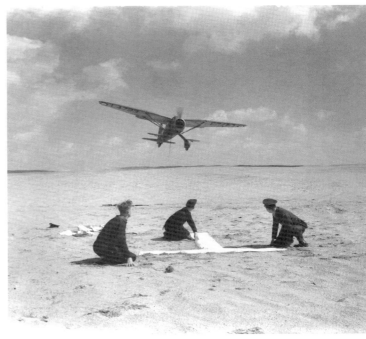

RIGHT A Lysander Mk II of No 208 Squadron parked at El Adem airfield, Libya, shortly after its occupation on 5 January 1941. In the foreground are the remains of one of 87 wrecked Italian aircraft found on the airfield. *(IWM ME RAF 576)*

BELOW An RAF Lysander flies over a convoy of lorries during the retreat into Egypt, 26 June 1942. *(IWM E13767)*

Even after the arrival of Field Marshal Rommel in the Western Desert and the subsequent British withdrawal, the Lysanders played a more than useful role in identifying the location of friendly forces, allowing a more orderly retreat than would otherwise have been possible. By now Lysanders from No 6 Squadron were heavily involved in Egypt and Libya, and during the rearguard defence of Tobruk their patrols were able to identify the position of enemy units so that RAF bombers could be directed to attack them by night.

RAF Lysanders of No 237 (Rhodesian) Squadron, based in the Sudan, also played an important part in General Platt's offensive against the Italians in Eritrea. In the decisive attack at Keren in March 1941 they carried out tactical, photographic and artillery reconnaissance, as well as turning their hand to the role of dive-bombers on occasion.

In the time between the success over the Italians and the onset of the much greater desert struggle against Rommel, events in Greece and later in Syria called the attention of the Lysander squadrons away from the desert and effectively ended their role as army cooperation aircraft. The Greco-Italian

war, which had begun in October 1940 with an invasion of Greek territories by Mussolini's forces, came swiftly to an end in April 1941 when German troops swept through Bulgaria and Yugoslavia to settle the conflict in favour of their Italian allies. The British response was to counter the German invasion by sending Commonwealth troops, which could hardly be spared from the Desert War, across the eastern Mediterranean to Greece. The Lysander pilots of No 208 Squadron, who were sent in support, soon found themselves an easy target for German Bf 109s and 110s, and on 22 April, barely a week after their arrival, they were withdrawn from the battlefront with six of their nine Lysanders destroyed.

Fortunately a large proportion of the crews of the wrecked aircraft survived and were able to return to Egypt. Their squadron was re-formed in Gaza in Palestine in time for the Allied invasion of Vichy French-controlled Syria. Here, Lysanders of No 208 Squadron helped in coordinating the advance of the military convoys during the short-lived campaign which achieved a Syrian surrender on 14 July 1941. Although the squadron returned to the Western Desert with a handful of Lysanders in November of

RIGHT No 28
Squadron's Lysander
Mk II, P1273, 'BF-J',
over the inhospitable
landscape of the
North-West Frontier
in 1942. (Andy Thomas
collection)

that year, the last of them had been withdrawn
within three months. No 6 Squadron finally
discarded the last of its Lysanders when they
were moved to Iraq early in 1942.

There was an RAF use for Lysanders further
east until there, too, the spread of Hawker
Hurricanes rendered them obsolete as a front-
line aircraft. Two squadrons, Nos 20 and 28,
were stationed in north-west India to patrol
the troublesome North-West Frontier, and
these were supported by No 1 Squadron
of the Indian Air Force who, along with their
RAF counterparts, took delivery of Lysanders
in the late summer of 1941, and operated

from Peshawar. When the Japanese bombed
Pearl Harbor in December 1941 and almost
immediately began their advance on India
through Malaya and Burma, the two RAF
squadrons were sent east to the India–Burma
border to assist the Allied forces retreating
through the jungle. IAF No 1 Squadron also
joined the war on the eastern front at Toungoo
once they had been able to train up sufficient
air gunners to fly as Lysander crew. (There
had been no need for them on the North-West
Frontier, where there was no threat from the air.)

All three squadrons found their main task
was that of bombing enemy positions, with

RIGHT Many hands
are required to remove
the fuselage of a
Lysander delivered
for use by the RAF's
No 1433 Flight, which
was based at Ivato in
Madagascar to fight
the Vichy French in
1942. (RAF Museum)

some involved in the defence of Rangoon while others were detailed to support the Chinese Fifth Army at the northern Burmese town of Lashio. The Lysanders suffered a number of casualties thanks to their own bombs, which, being of American make, did not fit well into the stub-wing bomb racks. Several fell from the aircraft as they taxied or while they were taking off, with severe consequences for their crews. The use of Lysanders over Burma was short-lived, however. By the end of 1942 Hurricanes had taken over all their front-line duties of both the Indian and the RAF squadrons.

The entry of the Japanese into the war brought about another far-flung task for RAF Lysanders, this time off the East African coast. The massive island of Madagascar was an outpost of Vichy France, and the British government was concerned that they would offer it to the Japanese as a stepping-off point for an invasion of Africa. As with Syria, the British planned a pre-emptive strike to take control of Madagascar, the execution of which began in May 1942. The British met with little resistance in the north of the island, where they established themselves in the area around

ABOVE Ground crew load bombs on to a Lysander in Madagascar. *(RAF Museum)*

LEFT RAF ground crew at work overhauling a Lysander in Madagascar. The removable access panels on the tailplane and along the fuselage are evident in this photograph. *(RAF Museum)*

Diego Suarez and where a flight of eight army cooperation Lysanders (No 1433), shipped in from the Middle East, was based. When the campaign to subdue the rest of the island began in September the flight was moved closer to the capital, Tananarive, and carried out seven sorties which involved strafing French gun positions in support of the Allied troops advancing on the town. Although the flight remained in Madagascar after the capital had been taken, by the time an armistice had been signed with the Vichy French in November 1942 the Lysanders had been withdrawn. On the rough landing grounds of the region they had been suffering particularly badly from shattered tail wheels, a problem that had dogged the aircraft throughout its wartime career.

It is probably fair to say that the Lysander, for all its unique slow-flying capabilities, its widespread use (around 1,600 were built altogether), and the obvious bravery of the very young men who flew them in cooperation with their often beleaguered army colleagues on the ground, would not have left much of a mark on the history of aerial warfare without the role for which it became famous after the war. At the time when the design was being withdrawn from RAF squadrons across the globe, a flight of Lysanders, which soon became a squadron, was just getting into its stride in a vital role about which only very few within the RAF had any idea. Its work is the subject of a later chapter. This chapter should conclude its study of the Lysander's less secret activities by giving a brief account of the occasions that the Lysander appeared in colours other than those of the RAF.

Perhaps the most surprising distinguishing mark to be seen on the wing of a Lysander is a swastika. This was not the Nazi version, but the Finnish emblem used for its original significance as a good-luck symbol on all the country's military aircraft between 1918 and 1945. Accounts vary somewhat as to how many

ABOVE Lysander Mk I, LY-133, LLv30, Finnish Air Force, 1940. *(Andy Thomas collection)*

LEFT Ski-equipped Lysander Mk I, LY-119, LLv16, Finnish Air Force, late 1942. *(Andy Thomas collection)*

ABOVE Lysander Mk II P1738, JAM Contingent, Cameroon, 1940. *(Andy Thomas collection)*

Lysanders were acquired by Finland, but the consensus is around 12. They were ordered at the time of the invasion of the country by Russia in November 1939 and arrived not long before the ensuing peace treaty signed in March 1940. Used for reconnaissance, photography, leaflet dropping and nuisance bombing, it is not clear whether they were ever used in action against the Allies when Finland sided with Germany later in the war.

If the Lysander was an enemy to the Vichy French in Syria and Madagascar, it was the friend of the Free French in General de Gaulle's campaigns to secure territory in northern and west Africa. Some 24 Lysanders were shipped out to the Free French Air Force based in Egypt in 1940. They were then moved south-west, with one group stationed at Fort Lamy (now N'Djamana) on the Cameroon/Chad border. Here they ran supply missions for the infantry

during two campaigns against the Italians in 1942 when Free French control was gained in the Fezzan region, now a part of southern Libya. In August 1942 six other Lysanders were distributed along the west African coast, at Pointe-Noire in the Congo, at Libreville in Gabon and at Douala in Cameroon, where they were tasked with hunting U-boats in the gulf of Guinea as well as providing a postal service for the area.

Unfortunately, little is known about how some other countries who ordered Lysanders just before the war made use of the aircraft. Egypt was one, paying £5,600 for each of its 19 Mk Is in 1938, and Turkey was another, taking delivery of 36 in early 1940. The Republic of Ireland took on 6 Lysanders in the summer of 1940 and Portugal were sent 8 Mk IIIAs which had come out of RAF service in September 1943.

The US Army Air Force made use of some 25 RAF Lysanders, mostly in the period leading up to D-Day to provide assistance for their gunnery schools. Canada, however, had a far greater interest in the aircraft to the extent that

the government there decided in 1938 to build their own versions of the plane at a factory in Hamilton, Ontario. In all, 225 Perseus-engined Canadian versions were built, a few of which were sent to Europe to equip their No 110 Squadron, based at Odiham, Hampshire, from June 1940. The pilots and crews of this squadron were some of the most flamboyant aviators ever seen in British airspace. Before the grim realities of the Battle of France locals would be astonished to hear cries of glee from above and to see figures hanging outside the Lysander lashed to the wing struts, their feet on the stub wings! While one other Royal Canadian Air Force squadron using Lysanders (No 414) was formed in the UK at Croydon in August 1941, the majority of the Canadian-built Lysanders were used to equip four army cooperation squadrons operating in Canada itself. Conditions in Canada meant that a heating system had to be installed in the cockpit and canopy of the plane. Much of the work for these Lysanders was target-towing for training Commonwealth aircrew, a vital role for the RCAF throughout the war.

ABOVE Lysander Mk I, Y511 'GF-U' of No 1 Squadron, Royal Egyptian Air Force, 1941. *(Andy Thomas collection)*

BELOW Conditions in Canada were such that a cockpit heating system was installed in Lysanders operating over the frozen North American wastes. This aircraft is being refuelled. *(IWM CAN 435)*

RIGHT Anti-invasion experiment No 1: Westland engineers demonstrate the strafing capabilities of the 'pregnant perch' and its ventral gun in a mocked-up fuselage. *(AgustaWestland)*

VARIATIONS ON A THEME

If, to some observers, the Lysander had an ungainly appearance and was sometimes known as 'the flying carrot', Westland also experimented with two further variants of the design which would give the nickname inventors yet more scope. With defence against German invasion a top priority after Dunkirk in 1940, thoughts had turned at Westland to giving the Lysander the ability to strafe attacking troops from the air. The resultant design (below), with its ventral bulge to house downward-pointing guns, soon became known as 'the pregnant perch'. The concept did get off the ground to the extent that an aircraft was built and test flown. Unfortunately, however, the engine failed during one of these flights and

RIGHT The demise of the 'pregnant perch': a soldier guards the wrecked experimental version of the Lysander (L4673) with downward-pointing gun, which made an emergency landing after suffering engine trouble while flying over Cornwall. *(Shuttleworth Collection)*

the aircraft crashed after making an emergency uphill landing in a Cornish field, close to some power cables. While the test pilot, George Snarey, escaped unhurt the design project itself did not survive the mishap.

Another Westland attempt to make the Lysander a more aggressive aircraft was the tandem-winged prototype built in 1941, influenced by a similar concept by the French designer Maurice Delanne and pictured below. The incongruous enlarged tailplane with end-plate fins and rudders allowed a Frazer Nash gun turret to be mounted at the rear of the fuselage in a style more reminiscent of a heavy bomber. Although this one-off version, with its plywood and Perspex mock-up turret, performed satisfactorily during test flying, the idea of its adoption as a night-fighter did not progress further than this single experimental aircraft.

ABOVE LEFT AND ABOVE Anti-invasion experiment No 2: Westland's test pilot Harald Penrose test-flying the tandem-wing Lysander prototype in 1941. The first prototype (K6127) was fitted with a new rear fuselage that was shortened to end in a power-operated turret, and supporting a wide-span tandem wing with large twin fins and rudders. The aircraft performed well but did not progress beyond this single experimental version. (*AgustaWestland*)

LEFT Anti-invasion experiment No 3: this trial configuration for the Lysander featured a Boulton-Paul four-gun power-operated turret, which only reached the mock-up stage. (*AgustaWestland*)

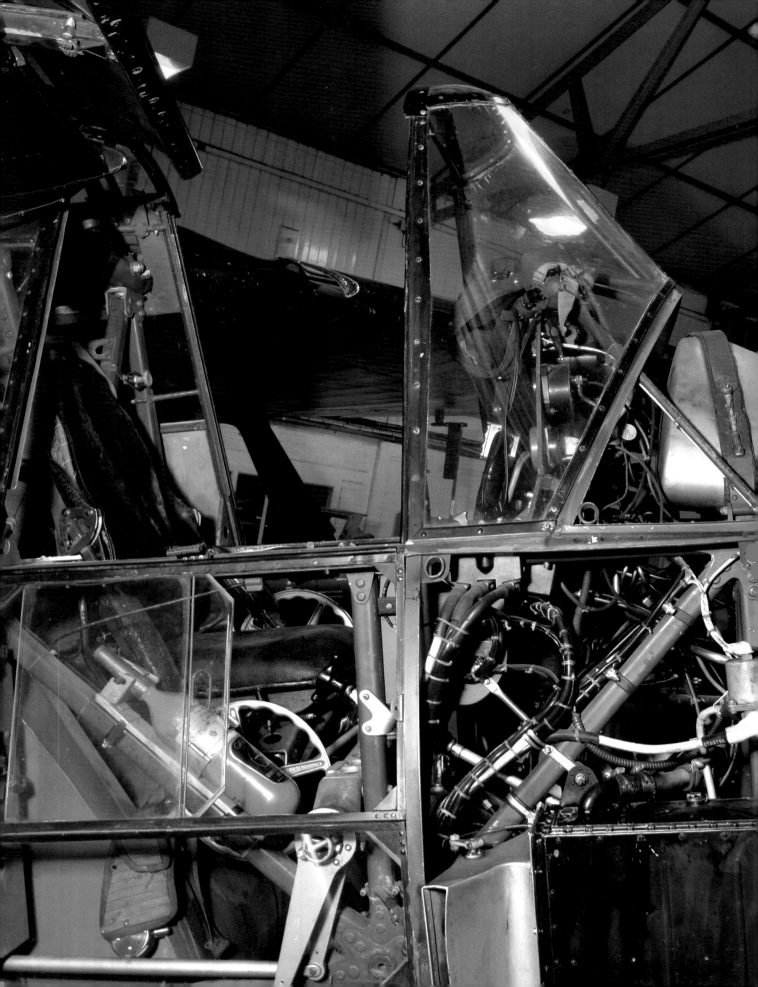

Chapter Three

Anatomy of the Lysander

The ability of the Lysander to fly slowly enough to land and pull up in less than the length of a football pitch came about through its unique leading-edge retracting slats and linked wing-flaps. This chapter allows the reader to understand their operation and gives details on all the design features of the aircraft and its powerplant.

OPPOSITE The Shuttleworth Lysander with inspection panels removed, showing the starboard side interior of the front cockpit, oil tank (silver-coloured, top centre behind the instrument panel), oil cooler air duct (silver-coloured, centre bottom), and the rear section of the Bristol Mercury engine. *(All photos John Harding unless credited otherwise)*

ABOVE The high parasol wing is the distinguishing feature of the Lysander.

RIGHT In this head-on view the Bristol Mercury radial engine and three-blade two-pitch propeller can be clearly seen.

Overview

The Lysander is a two-seat, single-engine, high-wing monoplane. The Mk I was fitted with an 890hp Bristol Mercury XII engine. The Mk II had a 905hp Bristol Perseus and all the remaining Mk IIIs were fitted with the 870hp Bristol Mercury XX engines. The propeller is a three-blade, two-pitch airscrew.

The engine mounting and the front part of the fuselage are constructed of square- and some round-section steel tubes. The rear portion is built up of round steel tubes, the aircraft being all metal apart from the wooden fairing formers (giving the rear fuselage its aerodynamic shape) and the fabric which covers the airframe.

The undercarriage is of the fixed cantilever type with oleo-pneumatic shock-absorber wheels enclosed by metal fairings (sometimes referred to as spats). A castoring tail wheel with a self-earthing tyre is carried in an assembly incorporating a shock-absorber leg.

The front cockpit is enclosed by a transparent structure with sliding doors; the rear cockpit is similarly covered but with a sliding roof. The pilot's seat has a harness with shoulder straps and the rear seat has leg straps only.

The fuel tank is behind the pilot's seat and the oil tank is mounted behind a fireproof bulkhead at the rear of the engine. Two oil coolers that also serve as cockpit heaters are fitted in the system.

The wings are attached at their root ends to the forward section of the fuselage and are supported by front and rear lift struts shackled to the undercarriage legs. The thickness and the chord of the wings both taper outboard and inboard of the lift strut joints. Slats are fitted along the entire length of the wings' leading edges. The trailing edges carry the ailerons and the flaps. The tailplane and fin are of monocoque construction and, along with the wings, ailerons, elevators and rudder, are fabric-covered.

Lysanders which were fitted out for army cooperation duty carried two fixed Browning guns, one within each wheel fairing. These were fired pneumatically by pressing a button on the pilot's control column spade grip. The requisite compressed air was derived from a container that also served the wheel brake and

ABOVE The heavily glazed cockpit coupé gives the pilot a good all-round view, enhanced by the high seating position inside the cockpit.

LEFT Wings taper outboard and inboard of the lift strut joints.

Westland Lysander

Mk III cutaway. *(Mike Badrocke)*

1 Fabric-covered elevator construction
2 Starboard tailplane construction
3 Elevator torque shaft
4 Elevator hinge control
5 Rudder operating lever
6 Tail navigation light
7 Fabric-covered rudder construction
8 Sternpost
9 Tailfin construction
10 Sloping fin spar
11 All-moving tailplane trim screw jack
12 Rear fuselage tubular steel framework
13 Tailplane centre-section carry-through
14 Tailplane pivot fixing
15 Sealing plate
16 Tail wheel leg strut
17 Castoring tail wheel
18 Tail lifting point
19 Fuselage frame-and-stringer side panelling
20 Starter handle stowage
21 Ballast weights
22 Fin leading edge ribs
23 Port elevator
24 Aerial lead-in
25 Flare launch tube
26 Control locking equipment stowage
27 Starboard side fuselage access panel
28 Fuselage turtle-deck construction
29 Observer's canopy cover, open
30 Trailing aerial winch
31 Twin Browning 0.303in (7.7mm) machine guns (Lysander IIIA)
32 Ammunition feed chutes
33 Vickers 'K' gun (early Lysander III)
34 Ammunition drum
35 Cartridge case collector bag
36 Rocking gun mounting pedestal
37 Spare ammunition drums
38 Rear canopy rail
39 Radio equipment
40 Radio power supply unit
41 'Push-in' boarding step
42 Battery
43 Wing tubular rear spar
44 Starboard flap
45 Aileron control mechanism
46 Wing lattice rib construction
47 Aileron tab
48 Starboard aileron
49 Inter-spar diagonal bracing struts
50 Wing-tip fairing
51 Starboard navigation light
52 Leading edge slat, open position
53 Slat guide rails
54 Leading edge rib construction
55 Double tapered front spar
56 Starboard wing struts
57 Fuselage fabric covering
58 Ventral bomb aiming position
59 Drift sight
60 Gunner's folding footrest
61 Signal cartridge stowage
62 Observer's swivelling seat
63 Parachute stowage
64 Cockpit central glazing
65 Centre section cabane struts
66 Chart table

67 Main fuel tank, capacity 95 Imp gal (432l)
68 Tailplane control rods
69 Forward fuselage tubular steel construction
70 Extended exhaust silencer (SAS aircraft)
71 Long-range fuel tank, capacity 150 Imp gal (682l)
72 Retractable message hook
73 0.303in (7.7mm) Browning machine gun
74 Wheel spat tail fairing access panel
75 Stub wing construction
76 120lb (54kg) HE bomb
77 Universal stores carrier
78 Parachute supply container
79 20lb (9kg) HE bombs
80 Light stores carrier
81 Dowty internally sprung wheel hub
82 Starboard mainwheel
83 Mainwheel spat fairing
84 Landing lamp
85 Machine-gun muzzle
86 Access step
87 One-piece main undercarriage leg strut
88 Ammunition feed chutes
89 Leg strut fairing
90 Wing bracing strut attachment joint
91 Ammunition boxes, 500 rounds per gun
92 Pilot's seat adjusting handwheel

93 Control column
94 Rudder pedals
95 Cockpit heater duct
96 Oil cooler exhaust louvres
97 Oil cooler
98 Engine bay fireproof bulkhead
99 Engine accessory equipment bay
100 Cowling air flaps
101 Exhaust pipe (Lysander III)
102 Port main undercarriage leg strut
103 Port mainwheel
104 Wheel spat fairing
105 Port landing lamp
106 Carburettor air intake
107 Oil cooler air duct
108 Propeller reduction gearbox
109 Cowling mounting struts
110 Propeller hub pitch change mechanism
111 Spinner
112 de Havilland three-blade variable-pitch propeller
113 Exhaust collector ring
114 Detachable engine cowling panels
115 Bristol Mercury XX nine-cylinder radial engine
116 Engine mounting ring
117 Oil tank
118 Windscreen panels
119 Reflector sight
120 Back of instrument panel
121 Control column handgrip
122 Pilot's seat
123 Safety harness
124 Crash axe stowage
125 Vertically sliding side window panels
126 Sliding cockpit roof hatch
127 Instrument panel light
128 Seat back armoured bulkhead
129 Centre section roof glazing

130 Wing spar/cabane strut attachment joint
131 Port side fixed boarding ladder (Mk IIIA SAS aircraft only)
132 Fabric-covered flap construction
133 Aerial mast
134 Flap/slat interconnection
135 Flap hydraulic jack
136 Slat guide rail
137 Aileron control tie rod (within rear strut)
138 Inboard leading edge slat, open
139 Port wing bracing struts
140 Strut attachment joint

141 Slat pneumatic damper
142 Flap/slap outboard interconnection
143 Aileron tab
144 Aileron control quadrant
145 Ventral pitot tube
146 Outboard slat pneumatic damper
147 Slat torque shaft
148 Leading edge aluminium skin panelling
149 Outboard slat, open position
150 Slat guide rails
151 Wing panel fabric covering
152 Port fabric-covered aileron
153 Wing tip fairing
154 Port navigation light

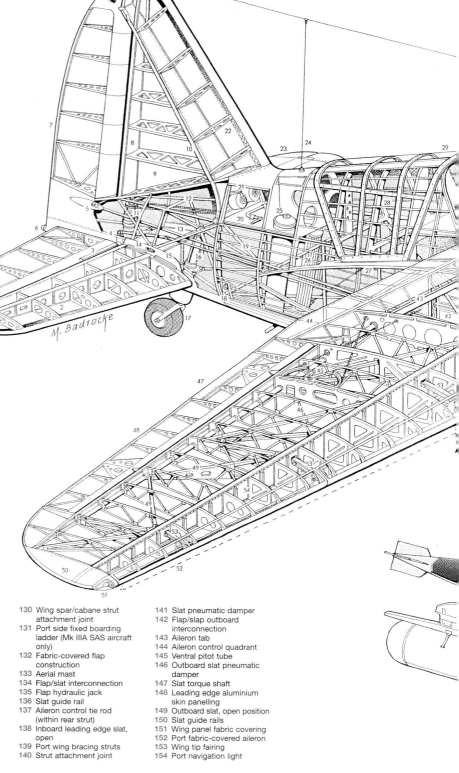

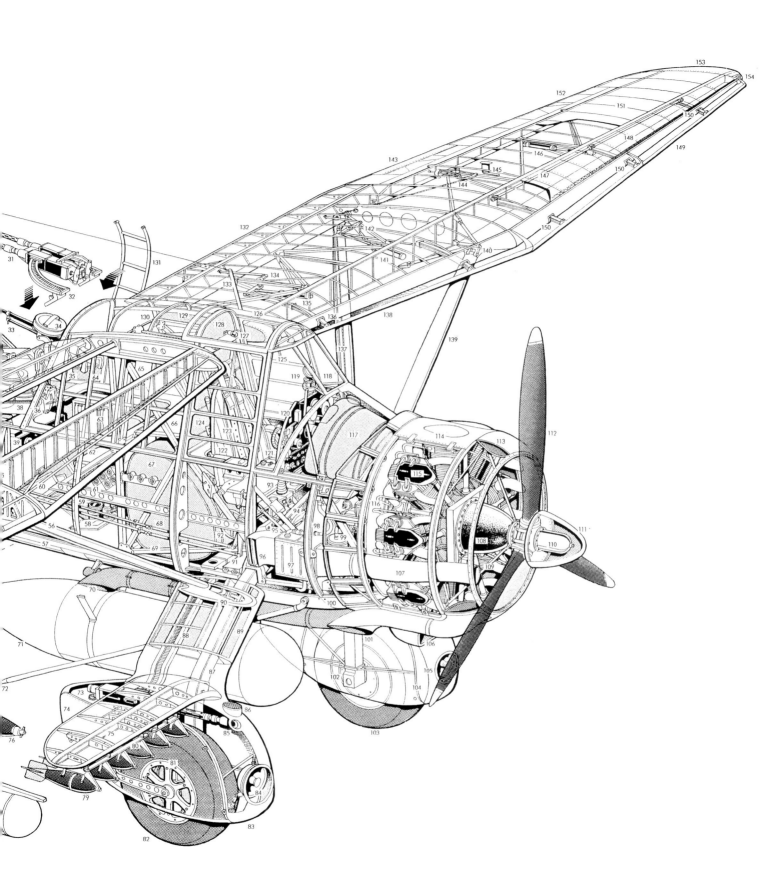

ABOVE The primary
fuselage structure is
built almost entirely
from steel tubing.
(Shuttleworth Collection)

Power for starting the engine is supplied by an
onboard accumulator.

Fuselage

For convenience of manufacture and
maintenance, the structure of the fuselage
is divided into three parts – the engine
mounting, the front fuselage portion and a rear
portion that includes the tail structure of the
fuselage. These parts are bolted together on
assembly to form an integral structure.

Engine mounting

The engine mounting consists of an aluminium-
alloy ring that is supported by a tubular
structure attached to the fuselage. At its forward
end the structure terminates in four extensions
that provide for bolted attachment of the engine
ring. At each attachment point on the ring are
a flanged bush and a washer, riveted together.
The main members of the engine mounting
structure are square-section steel tubes; the
cross bracings in the side and top bays are
square-section aluminium-alloy tubes and the
bracing in the bottom bay is a welded steel
tubular framework. The fireproof bulkhead

the camera gun systems. A Lewis gun was
mounted on a pillar in the rear cockpit.

An engine-driven generator provides
electrical power for all navigation, identification
and cockpit lighting as well as gun heating.
Short-wave R/T radio communication is
provided by a receiver and transmitter mounted
in crates at the back of the rear cockpit.

RIGHT Fuselage
structure showing
the three principal
sections, spars and
attachment points.
(Shuttleworth Collection)

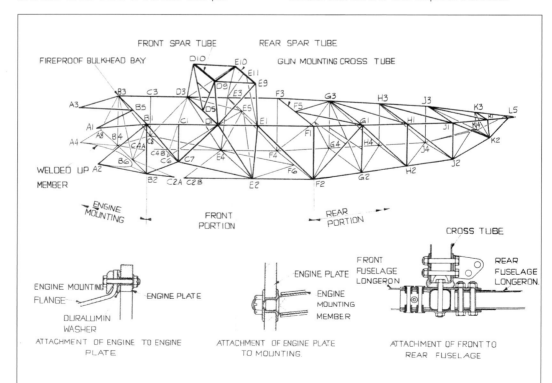

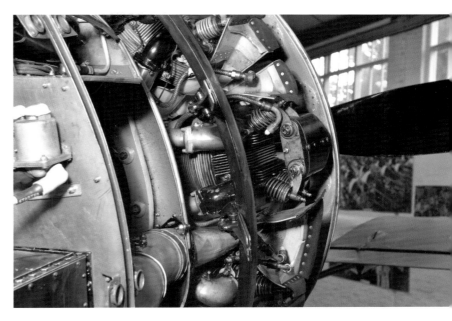

RIGHT Engine mounting ring and engine bay fireproof bulkhead (foreground).

consists of asbestos sheeting sandwiched between two aluminium panels. A removable door in the bulkhead allows withdrawal of the engine-starting motor.

The engine is fitted with an aerodynamic long-chord cowl, the rear portion of which has controllable gills for cooling. Cowling catches fitted to channels fixed to the longerons and to the nosepiece carried on the engine mounting plate provide attachment for the cowling panels of the front fuselage. The edges of the panels, where they are in contact with the fuselage, are sealed by rubber inserts cemented in the channel formers. The edges of the cowling panels are reinforced by riveted-on extrusions. Forward of the fireproof bulkhead, the panels are of aluminium. The panels covering the portion of the fuselage to the rear of the bulkhead around the forward part of the pilot's cockpit are of magnesium-alloy. These are detachable, held to the rubber-lined channel formers by quick-release fasteners.

Front fuselage

The front portion of the fuselage extends from the fireproof bulkhead to the back of the rear cockpit and carries the attachment fittings for the wings, undercarriage legs and rear fuselage. It also contains the pilot's cockpit, the fuel tank and several items of equipment. It is a rigidly braced structure of steel and aluminium-alloy tubes joined by gusset plates or U-section extrusions that are secured by bolts or by ferrules and rivets. There is a superstructure to the front fuselage that is positioned between the front and rear cockpits, and the wings are attached to root end joints at the top of this superstructure. Most of the joints in the front fuselage are similar in construction and have brackets shaped to suit the joint. These brackets, together with inner and outer steel sideplates, are used for connecting the individual members of the fuselage to their respective joints.

The windscreen front portion of the pilot's coupé consists of a welded framework, safety-glass centre panel and shaped, transparent top

VITAL STATISTICS

Dimensions

Wingspan:	50ft (15.24m).
Height:	14ft 6in (4.42m).
Length overall:	30ft 6in (9.30m).
Wing area:	260ft^2 (24.16m^2).
Wing chord:	6ft 8in (2.03m).

Weights

Empty:	4,065lb (1,843kg).
Loaded:	5,920lb (2,685kg).
Maximum permissible:	7,500lb (3,401kg).

Tankage

Fuel capacity:	87 gallons (396 litres).
Oil capacity:	7 gallons (32 litres).

Performance

Maximum speed (Mk I):	229mph (369kph) at 10,000ft (3,048m), 224mph (360kph) at 15,000ft (4,572m).
Maximum diving speed:	300mph (483kph).
Minimum speed, engine on (Mk I):	55mph (89kph).
Range at economical cruising speed of 150mph (241kph):	500 miles (805 km).
Take-off run to unstick:	165yd (151m).
Take-off run to clear 50ft (15.24m) obstacle:	230yd (210m) (Mk I); 245yd (224m) (Mk II).
Service ceiling:	26,500ft (8,100m).

RIGHT Front fuselage showing undercarriage member and fuselage joints. A – boss for bolts securing member to fuselage; B – for fittings securing the lift strut shackles; C – for the attachments for the bomb wings. *(Shuttleworth Collection)*

BELOW Typical front fuselage joint. *(Shuttleworth Collection)*

BELOW RIGHT Transparent coupé coverings and windscreen. *(Shuttleworth Collection)*

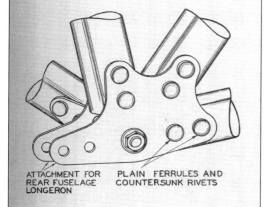

ATTACHMENT FOR REAR FUSELAGE LONGERON

PLAIN FERRULES AND COUNTER.SUNK RIVETS

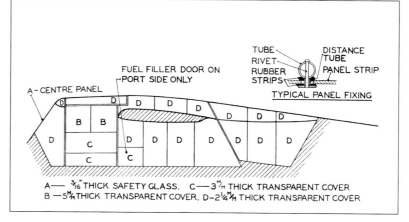

FUEL FILLER DOOR ON PORT SIDE ONLY

TUBE
RIVET
RUBBER STRIPS

DISTANCE TUBE
PANEL STRIP

TYPICAL PANEL FIXING

A – CENTRE PANEL

A—³⁄₁₆" THICK SAFETY GLASS. C—3" THICK TRANSPARENT COVER
B—5" THICK TRANSPARENT COVER. D–2¼" THICK TRANSPARENT COVER

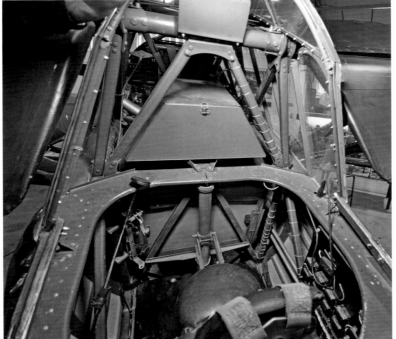

ABOVE LEFT A cross-tube at the top of the windscreen framework aids the pilot when entering or leaving the cockpit.

ABOVE Pilot's seat in the front cockpit.

LEFT The crew position in the rear cockpit.

BELOW LEFT Behind the rear cockpit is stowage for compressed air bottles for the brake system.

BELOW The rear cockpit roof can be easily slid open or closed and is held in place by a single locking handle.

RIGHT Removable panels give access to the interior of the starboard fuselage. *(AgustaWestland)*

OPPOSITE Inside the rear fuselage looking aft showing wooden longerons and framing, and steel tubing.

BELOW Inside the rear fuselage top fairing looking aft.

BELOW RIGHT Rear fuselage tubular framework.

and side panels. A cross-tube at the top of the framework serves as a handrail for the pilot when entering or leaving the cockpit. The fuselage superstructure between the two cockpits is enclosed by a transparent covering held in place by a fixed wood and welded steel framework. Vertical sliding doors on the sides of the pilot's coupé consist of a series of extruded frames and transparent panels. The doors are opened or closed from the outside by pushing back a horizontal sliding panel at the top of the door and pulling a leather tab that operates the bolts. Both the front and the rear cockpits have sliding roofs. A catch in the windscreen framework holds the pilot's roof in position during flight, when it may be either open or closed. The rear cockpit roof can easily be opened or closed under all flight conditions and is held in position by a single locking handle on the starboard side.

Rear fuselage

The rear portion, extending from the back of the rear cockpit to the tail, is built up of round steel tubes welded at the joints. The top longerons taper gradually both in plan and elevation until the final section, where they taper more sharply towards the single joint at the tail. Fittings are incorporated at various joints for the attachment of the fin, the tailplane together with its adjusting gear, the tail wheel, the bomb carrier, the fairings and items of equipment. Fabric covers a framework of wooden stringers that forms the fairing for the rear fuselage as well as the rear end of the front fuselage. The fairing at the starboard side has large removable fabric-covered panels to give access to the equipment. There are further inspection doors on the port side fairing. The covering at the rear end of the fuselage around the tailplane and fin is composed of magnesium-

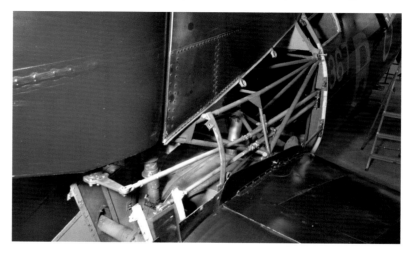

ANATOMY OF THE LYSANDER

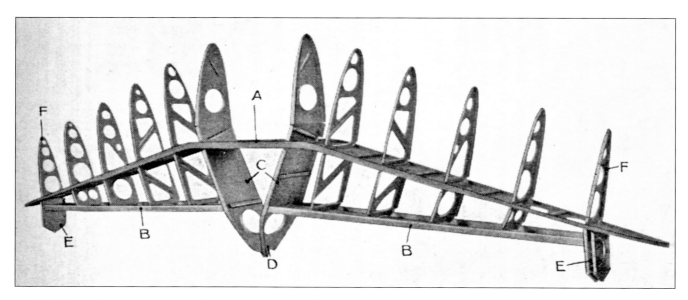

alloy panels that are held by cowling fasteners to a welded steel tubular framework. This framework is attached to the rear fuselage structure by bolts and clamps and is readily detachable.

Tail unit

The tail unit of the Lysander consists of a cantilever tailplane (*ie* with no external bracing), statically balanced elevators, a fin and a mass-balanced rudder. The tailplane is adjustable for incidence and is mounted at the rear of the fuselage. The elevators are hinged to the rear of the tailplane. The fin is attached to the top of the fuselage and carries the rudder at the rear. The top of the rudder is hinged to the fin and the bottom to the fuselage. The rear of the fuselage, both above and below the elevators, is enclosed in a streamline fairing that carries the tail navigation lamp.

Tailplane

The tailplane is of all-metal construction with a covering of Duralumin sheet, except for the removable tips, which are of aluminium. It is attached to the fuselage by two fittings on the top surface, located over the front spar. An aft extension of the centre portion carries a fitting

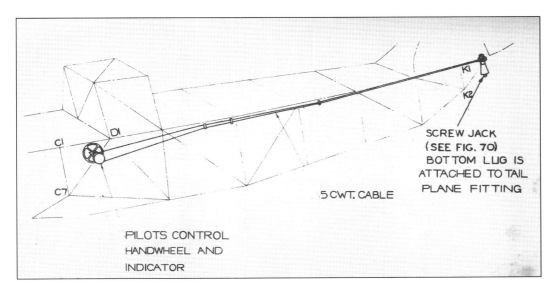

LEFT Tailplane adjusting gear control. *(Shuttleworth Collection)*

BELOW Tailplane incidence board and settings.

for attaching the tail-adjusting screw jack, the centre hinge bearing for the elevator, the adjustable stop for the elevator control lever and the incidence board locating peg.

Elevators

The elevators are connected at their inner ends by a centre hinge plate carried on a tubular extension riveted to the spar webs. The elevator control lever is attached to the centre hinge plates at the assembly of the elevators to the tailplane. The lead for the elevator static balance is carried in an adjustable weight-holder in the form of a tubular member mounted between

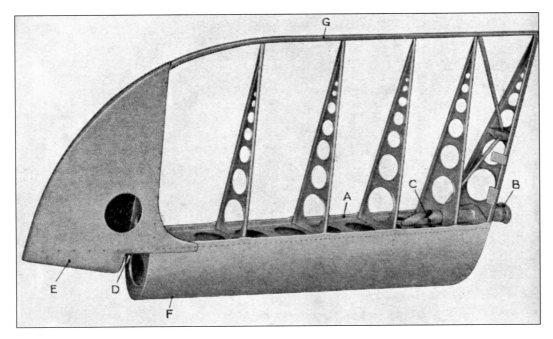

LEFT Skeleton view of the starboard elevator. The port elevator is identical, but handed. A – Duralumin channel section spars; B – centre hinge plate; C – tubular extension; D – outer hinge bearing; E – elevator tip; F – nosing; G – trailing edge. *(Shuttleworth Collection)*

RIGHT Elevator control mechanism. *(Shuttleworth Collection)*

BELOW Starboard side of the cockpit showing the elevator control transmission tube to which is attached the lever and rod (outermost); the inner lever and rod are for the rudder. Both sets of linkages are attached to the control column cast-aluminium alloy beam. *(Shuttleworth Collection)*

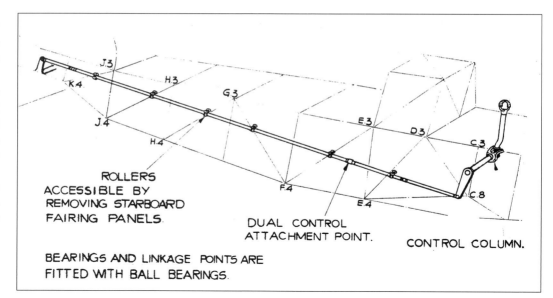

ROLLERS ACCESSIBLE BY REMOVING STARBOARD FAIRING PANELS.

DUAL CONTROL ATTACHMENT POINT.

CONTROL COLUMN.

BEARINGS AND LINKAGE POINTS ARE FITTED WITH BALL BEARINGS.

BELOW Fin skeleton showing:
A – front post;
B – rudder top hinge bearing;
C – aluminium false rear spar.
(Shuttleworth Collection)

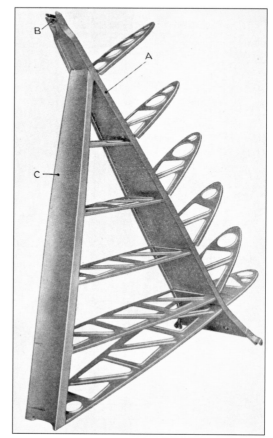

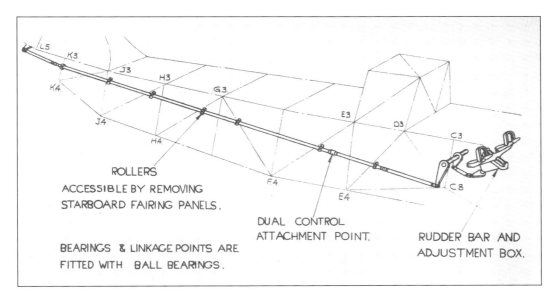

the two inboard nose ribs and the end rib at the rear of the nosing. The number of these small lead weights may be varied to suit the balance required. The nose ribs are covered with Duralumin sheet that forms the nosing. The elevator tip is of aluminium, welded at the trailing edge boundary. The trailing edge of the elevator consists of an aluminium U-section member into which the tips of the tail ribs are riveted. The elevators are completely covered in fabric.

Fin

The fin is of all-metal construction and when assembled to the fuselage is attached at three points, two at the front and one at the rear. A small cover plate is provided at the top of the aluminium fin tip; by removing this cover a spring-loaded aerial attachment for use with the fixed aerial may be withdrawn. The framework for the fin is made up of a series of aluminium-alloy booms joined by a Duralumin web fitted with stiffeners.

Rudder

The nose and tail ribs of the rudder are Duralumin plate pressings; the rudder post is of Duralumin channel-section running the full depth of the rudder. The rudder post has two hinge bearings, one bolted to the top of the channel and the other, together with an operating control lever, attached to a tubular extension of the post at the bottom. Below the tapered nosing at the top of the rudder a mass-balanced weight is carried inside the leading edge. The rudder is fabric-covered.

LEFT **Rudder bottom hinge and tailplane assembly.**

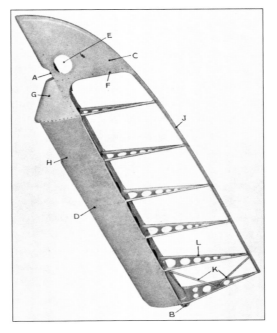

LEFT **Rudder skeleton. A – top hinge; B – bottom hinge; C – rudder tip; D – Duralumin sheet nosing; E – hole to give access for attachment of top hinge bearing; F – top nose rib; G – welded aluminium nosing; H – mass-balanced weight inside leading edge; J – trailing edge; K – two aluminium stabilising struts; L – rib.** *(Shuttleworth Collection)*

**ABOVE Starboard
wing skeleton.**
(AgustaWestland)

Wings

The wings or main planes of the Lysander are formed by a front and rear spar bridged by a series of 25 Duralumin ribs and braced by a system of parallel and diagonal struts. The wings are fitted with ailerons that have combined trim and servo tabs incorporated at the rear. Inboard and outboard slats are attached to the leading edges of each wing and flaps are fitted to the trailing edges inboard of the ailerons. The inboard slats are connected to the flaps and to an air damper in the port wing to govern the speed at which the slats operate. The outboard slats function independently and are each fitted with an air damper.

The flaps are entirely automatic and are operated by the inboard slat movements through a system of links, cables, levers and push-pull tubes, all of which are governed by the air damper in the port wing. The pilot is provided with a control that can lock the flaps.

**LEFT Slat attachment and adjustment
mechanism.** *(Shuttleworth Collection)*

BELOW Starboard wing flap.

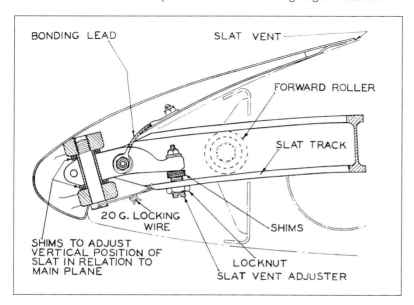

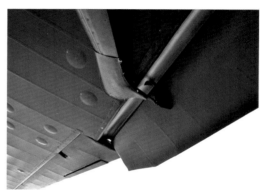

LEFT Main plane
– inboard bays. A –
bearing that carries
the inner operating
levers of the flaps; D –
cables for navigation
lamp carried in tubular
duct. *(Shuttleworth
Collection)*

The leading edges of the ailerons and flaps are shrouded by fabric masks attached to the wings' trailing edges.

The control cables and the leads of the various systems, such as the air-speed indicator, pass through the fairings and cuffs fitted to the two port and two starboard lift struts that support the front and rear spars of the wings.

Spars

The front spar is a built-up D-section Duralumin member and forms the leading edge along the whole length of the wing. The tubular rear spar has two parts that meet where they are attached to the rear lift strut. The tracks of the inner and outer slats are carried on brackets fixed to the rear of the spar.

Ribs

All the nose ribs are sheet Duralumin pressings with holes punched through to lighten them and bent flanges to add strength.

Wing

Fabric covers the framework of the wing, other than its leading edge. The operating levers for the flaps are housed within the wing structure, the inner one attached to a strut positioned alongside the fourth rib out from the wing root, and the other outboard of the point where the lift struts meet the spars. The air damper that serves both wings' inner slats is positioned close to the inner operating lever on the port wing. The outer slats' air dampers are fitted between the 18th and 19th ribs. The navigation lamp mounting and terminal block at the outboard end of the wing are enclosed by a transparent wing-tip nose fairing. The electrically heated pressure head of the airspeed indicator

BELOW Main plane
– lift strut bays. B –
bearing carrying outer
operating levers of
the flaps; C – aileron
control lever bearing;
D – cables in tubular
duct. *(Shuttleworth
Collection)*

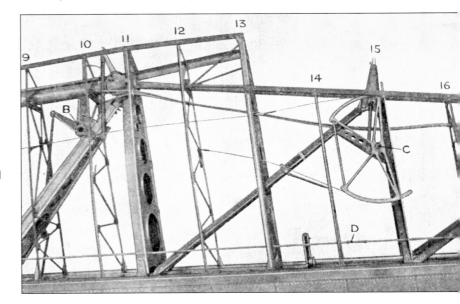

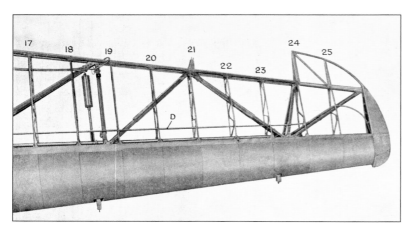

ABOVE Main plane – outboard bays. D – cables in tubular duct. *(Shuttleworth Collection)*

RIGHT Main plane – root end joints. A – drag struts; B – D-section front spar; C – rear tubular spar; D – extended arm forming flap hinge; E and F – wing to fuselage attachment fittings; G – eyebolts with rings for use when slinging main plane. *(Shuttleworth Collection)*

(the pitot tube) is mounted on the port wing near the aileron centre hinge.

Lift struts

The lower ends of the struts are pin-jointed to shackles attached to the undercarriage legs. The upper end of the front strut is pin-jointed to a shackle braced to the wing's front spar and the rear strut supports the wing at the point where the two-part rear spar is joined. The struts are of aluminium-alloy with Duralumin fairings on the leading and trailing edges.

RIGHT The lower ends of the lift struts are attached to the undercarriage legs.

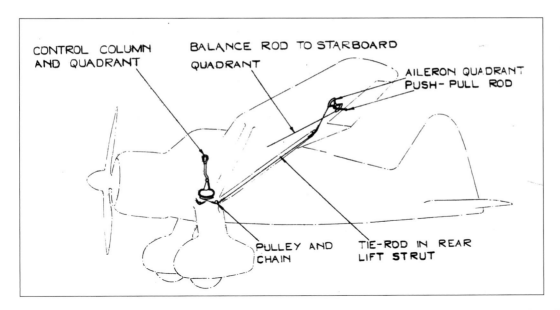

CONTROL COLUMN
AND QUADRANT

BALANCE ROD TO STARBOARD
QUADRANT

AILERON QUADRANT
PUSH-PULL ROD

PULLEY AND
CHAIN

TIE-ROD IN REAR
LIFT STRUT

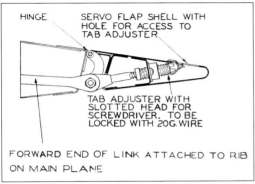

HINGE

SERVO FLAP SHELL WITH
HOLE FOR ACCESS TO
TAB ADJUSTER

TAB ADJUSTER WITH
SLOTTED HEAD FOR
SCREWDRIVER. TO BE
LOCKED WITH 20G. WIRE

FORWARD END OF LINK ATTACHED TO RIB
ON MAIN PLANE

ABOVE Aileron control mechanism.
(Shuttleworth Collection)

Ailerons and flaps

While the outboard ailerons are statically and
aerodynamically balanced, the inboard flaps are
only aerodynamically balanced. Both are similar
in construction with Duralumin sheeting on the
leading edge and fabric covering the rest of the
metal structure.

Slats

The outer slats on both wings operate
independently and are not interconnected. It
is the inner slats that operate the automatic
flaps, and the inner levers of both the port

RIGHT Top: inner slat tracks and interconnection;
bottom: outer slat tracks. *(Shuttleworth Collection)*

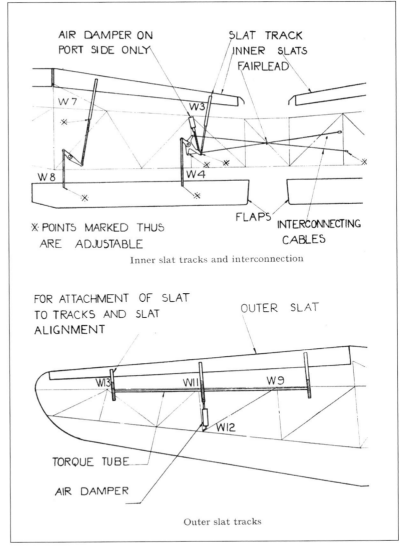

AIR DAMPER ON
PORT SIDE ONLY

SLAT TRACK
INNER SLATS
FAIRLEAD

W 7

W3

W 8

W 4

FLAPS

INTERCONNECTING
CABLES

X POINTS MARKED THUS
ARE ADJUSTABLE

Inner slat tracks and interconnection

FOR ATTACHMENT OF SLAT
TO TRACKS AND SLAT
ALIGNMENT

OUTER SLAT

W13

W11

W 9

W12

TORQUE TUBE

AIR DAMPER

Outer slat tracks

and starboard inner slats are connected by cables which cross over between the fuselage superstructure in order to ensure their movement is synchronised.

Landing gear

The undercarriage is attached to the front fuselage and consists of an inverted U-shaped member forming a pair of legs and two landing wheels incorporating oleo-

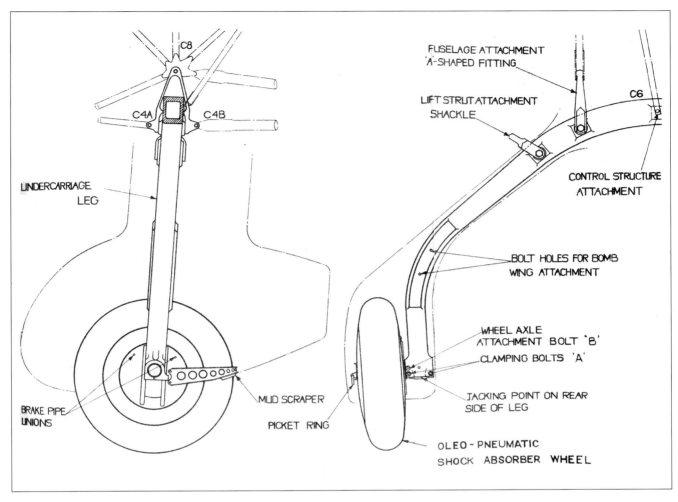

FUSELAGE ATTACHMENT
'A'-SHAPED FITTING

LIFT STRUT ATTACHMENT
SHACKLE

C6

CONTROL STRUCTURE
ATTACHMENT

BOLT HOLES FOR BOMB
WING ATTACHMENT

WHEEL AXLE
ATTACHMENT BOLT 'B'

CLAMPING BOLTS 'A'

JACKING POINT ON REAR
SIDE OF LEG

OLEO-PNEUMATIC
SHOCK ABSORBER WHEEL

C8

C4A   C4B

UNDERCARRIAGE
LEG

BRAKE PIPE
UNIONS

MUD SCRAPER

PICKET RING

pneumatic shock absorbers. The wheels have pneumatically operated brakes and mudscrapers. Metal fairings that carry the gun-heating ducts and ammunition chutes cover each leg. Further metal fairings are mounted over the wheels and carry a fixed Browning gun and a landing lamp. The lower ends of the lift struts are shackled to the undercarriage leg at the top. Detachable bomb-carrier wings, projecting above the undercarriage wheels, are attached to the legs. Covers are provided to seal the apertures in the leg fairings when the bomb wings are removed.

Undercarriage legs

The undercarriage is made of a single piece of aluminium-alloy, bent to form the legs and attached to the underside of the fuselage by two large bolts that fit into a casting connected to the bottom longerons. The upper ends of the trailing edge portions of the leg fairings are

ABOVE Undercarriage structure and attachment. *(Shuttleworth Collection)*

LEFT Detail of how the undercarriage attaches to the underside of the fuselage. *(Shuttleworth Collection)*

RIGHT A landing lamp
was fitted in the front
of each undercarriage
fairing.

Undercarriage wheels

The wheel assembly consists of a Dowty type shock-absorber unit which is free to slide in a vertical direction within the large half casting carrying the inboard boss of the wheel. The brakes are applied by a hand lever clamped to the pilot's control column spade grip. A cable links the lever to a relay valve mounted below the cockpit flooring and connected to the rudder bar. The relay valve distributes the pressurised air supply differentially to the port and starboard brake unit according to the position of the rudder bar. This helps the pilot to turn the aeroplane on the ground. The air supply to each brake unit is fed through pipelines that run through the leg fairings. The air supply is also used for the pneumatic operation of the guns and the camera.

Tail wheel

The tail wheel is fitted with a 5in by 12in tyre and is carried in a forked fitting at the lower end of an oleo-pneumatic shock-absorber unit. The shock absorber is similar to the one used in the undercarriage wheel except that

hinged to give access to the ammunition chute, the gun and brake pipelines, and the cables for the landing lamp and the bomb release mechanism.

RIGHT Port main
wheel with hub cover
in place.

RIGHT Port main
wheel with hub cover
removed to reveal
spoked wheel.

FAR RIGHT Castoring
tail wheel with Dunlop
twin-contact aero tyre
to stop shimmy.

the lower cylinder of the tail wheel strut is free to castor. There is a self-centring device that keeps the wheel in the line of flight when the Lysander is airborne. As soon as the leg is compressed on landing, the device automatically disengages.

Systems

Fuel

A 95-gallon fuel tank strapped in position between the front and rear cockpits feeds the system through a series of copper and flexible piping. The master fuel cock is controlled by a handle on the port coaming of the pilot's cockpit. Fuel from the tank sump is driven to the carburettor by an engine-powered pump. A fuel priming pump and a three-way priming cock are mounted on the pilot's instrument panel. Fuel is delivered to the priming connection of the carburettor and the engine through the three-way cock by manual operation of the priming pump. Two fuel pressure gauges on the instrument panel, connected by pipelines to the outlet sides of the

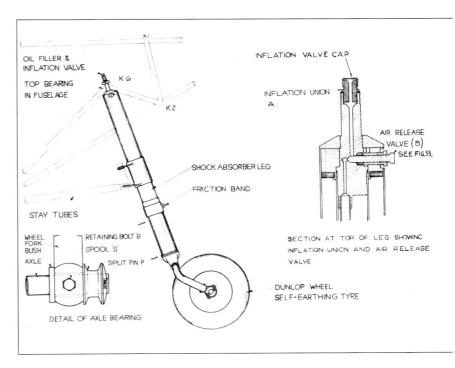

ABOVE Tail wheel shock absorber leg detail. *(Shuttleworth Collection)*

BELOW Fuel system schematic. *(Shuttleworth Collection)*

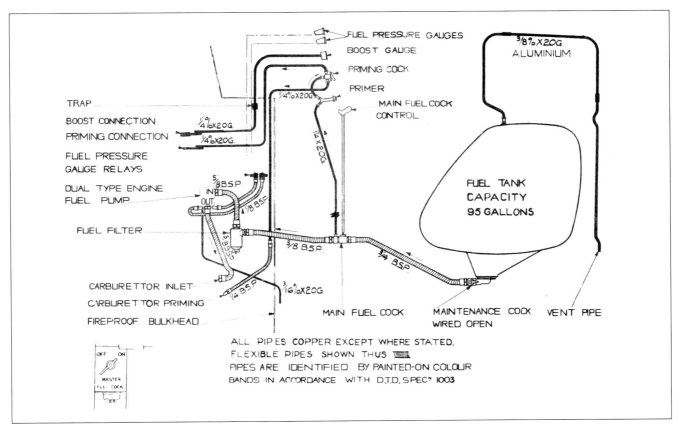

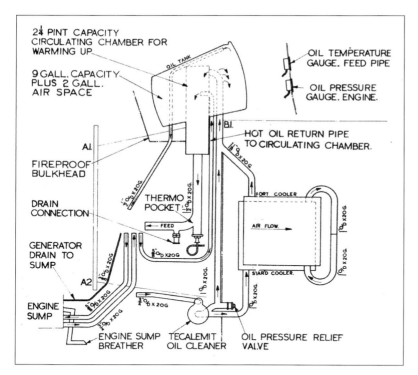

ABOVE **Oil system schematic.** (Shuttleworth Collection)

BELOW **Electrical wiring looms for navigation and landing lights, starter and battery on the starboard side of the cockpit.**

engine-driven pump, show the pressure of each section of the pump.

Oil

The oil tank is carried on top of the engine mounting structure behind the fireproof bulkhead. Metal pipes and rubber hose are used throughout the oil system. Oil is drawn by the engine pump from the tank circulating chamber and, after passing through the engine, is returned to the tank through the oil cleaner and the coolers. If the return oil pressure in the coolers exceeds 24 to 27psi the oil flows directly

into the tank through the pressure relief valve. For warming-up, hot oil is returned direct to the tank circulating chamber, whence it is again transferred to the engine via the feed pipe at the bottom of the tank. An overflow pipe at the top of the tank allows excess oil to flow back to the engine sump. The inlet temperature and the oil pressure at the engine are each recorded by gauges on the pilot's instrument panel.

Cockpit heating and cooling

The front and rear cockpits can be heated independently. Air ducts pass through oil coolers, one on the starboard side for the pilot and one on the port side for the rear cockpit. Manually operated flap valves regulate the warm air supply to the cockpits. A single control on the instrument panel allows the pilot to override the crew's heating requirement when the engine is warming up. Cold air, available only to the pilot, is channelled to the cockpit by means of a gauze-covered scoop on the port leg of the undercarriage.

Electrical

The electrical equipment provides services for lighting, landing lamps, navigation, signalling, camera motor, wireless motor-generator, engine starting, gun heating and bomb control. The power supply is derived from a 500W engine-driven generator positioned on the port side of the engine mounting. During flight, the generator charges both the general services accumulator and the starting accumulator, which are mounted in the rear fuselage on the port side of the rear cockpit floor. The distribution panel on the starboard side of the rear cockpit carries all the instruments and fuses.

Cockpit controls

Normally the Lysander is controlled from the pilot's cockpit, but provision has been made for the installation of dual controls in the rear cockpit.

Control column

A spade grip incorporating a gun-firing button, brake control and a parking lever is fitted to the top of the control column. The column operates both the ailerons and the elevators by a system

LEFT Overhead view down into the front cockpit showing the instrument panel and main controls.

of levers, pulleys, chain rollers, cables and rods which run through the framework of the wings for the ailerons and back through the fuselage for the elevators.

Rudder bar

A similar system links the foot-operated, pivoted rudder bar in the cockpit to the rudder. The bar is a single cast member, adjustable for leg reach, with foot-plates, heel-rests and leather toe straps. Cables anchored to the central boss, together with springs and pulleys, return the rudder bar to the aft position automatically when foot pressure is released.

Tailplane adjuster

The incidence of the tailplane to maintain longitudinal trim is controlled by a handwheel attached to the fuselage structure on the port side of the pilot's seat. Movement of the handwheel actuates a continuous run of cable linked to a screw jack mounted at the far end of the rear fuselage.

FAR LEFT Control column with gun button.

BELOW Rudder bar.

Propeller pitch adjuster

A red knob on the instrument panel controls the pitch of the propeller – pushed in for the fine pitch required for take-off and landing, pulled out for the coarse pitch setting required for cruising.

Throttle and mixture controls

These controls are mounted in the quadrant at the port side of the cockpit. The three positions for the throttle are marked 'SHUT', 'CRUISING' and 'RATED TAKE OFF'. The two positions for the automatic mixture control are marked 'NORMAL' and 'WEAK'. If the mixture control is in the 'WEAK' position, closing the throttle or opening it further than half its travel will return the mixture control to 'WEAK'. The knob of the throttle lever carries the bomb-firing push button.

Cowling gills control

The handle for the gill control is on the starboard side of the pilot's cockpit. The gills must be fully open for running up the engine, taxiing, taking off and climbing. In general, they should be closed (by turning the handle clockwise) while cruising.

Carburettor auxiliary controls

The carburettor slow-running cut-out controls on the engine are connected by cables to a control knob on the pilot's instrument panel. This is used only when stopping the engine.

Air intake control

This control admits warm air to the carburettor when starting the engine.

Engine starter button

This push button on the starboard side of the instrument panel is protected from inadvertent operation by a hinged cover. The starting motor should not be run for more than ten seconds at a time. Should the engine fail to start in ten seconds, the motor should be stopped and allowed to cool off for thirty seconds before another attempt to start is made.

Fuel cock

The fuel cock handle is on the port coaming of the cockpit. It has an 'ON' and 'OFF' position and allows fuel to flow from the tank behind the pilot's position.

Priming pump and cock

The priming cock has three positions: 'OFF', 'PRIME TO CARBURETTOR' and 'PRIME TO ENGINE'. When starting the engine, the carburettor must first be primed until a slight pressure is indicated on the fuel pressure gauge. The cock should then be turned to the engine priming position. In warm weather or when the engine is hot, two strokes of the priming pump plunger should be enough. In colder conditions, ten strokes may be needed.

Oil heating control

This knob on the instrument panel is pulled out to increase the temperature of the oil while running up the engine.

Identification lamps

These lamps can be switched on or off or operated by a Morse key (for signalling). The key is positioned below the wireless Morse key on the starboard side of the front cockpit. The upward-facing lamp is positioned on the roof of the fuselage superstructure and the downward one beneath the rear cockpit.

Landing lamps

Two landing lamps are mounted, one in each wheel fairing. They are operated independently by the pilot through a switch on the port side cockpit coaming, just aft of the fuel cock.

Intercommunication indicator lamps

The pilot is able to attract the attention of his crew member by a push-button switch on the starboard coaming that activates two lamps in the rear cockpit.

Armaments and other equipment

Guns

A Lysander fitted out for army cooperation purposes carried two fixed .303 Browning

guns, one mounted inside each of the main wheel fairings of the undercarriage. These were fired by the pilot using a button on the control column and a reflector-type gunsight, fitted with a sun screen and mounted above the instrument panel. Ammunition for each gun was carried in boxes with a 500-round capacity.

The Lewis .303 was carried on a rocking-pillar-type mounting attached to a fuselage crossmember below the sliding roof of the rear cockpit. Eight magazines of ammunition were provided for the Lewis gunner.

ABOVE Lysander Mk II R1999 of No 225 Squadron showing the rear cockpit with twin 0.303in Lewis guns for the observer. *(PRM Aviation Collection)*

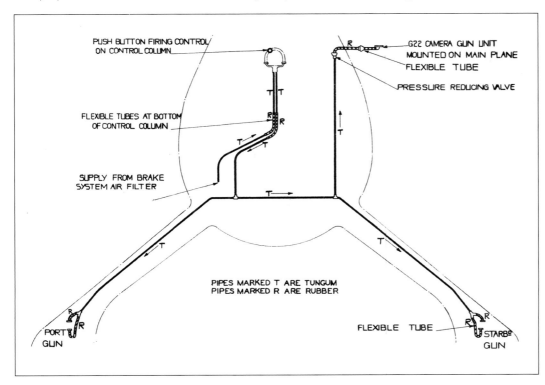

LEFT Gun and camera gun schematic. *(Shuttleworth Collection)*

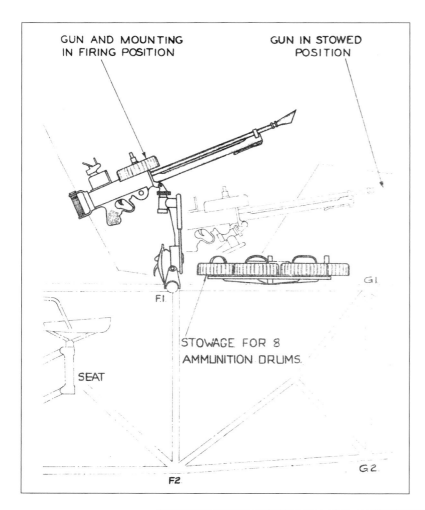

GUN AND MOUNTING
IN FIRING POSITION

GUN IN STOWED
POSITION

G.I.

F.I.

STOWAGE FOR 8
AMMUNITION DRUMS.

SEAT

F2

G.2.

ABOVE Rear Lewis gun mounting. *(Shuttleworth Collection)*

ABOVE The invasion fever that swept Britain in the summer of 1940 saw some Lysanders fitted with a 20mm cannon on each wheel fairing for ground strafing. This is a Lysander Mk II (P1684, 'UG-A') of No 16 Squadron at Cambridge in June–July 1940. *(Andy Thomas collection)*

RIGHT Detail of wheel spat and stub wing showing bomb shackles, landing lamp and aperture for the forward-firing 0.303in Browning machine gun (one of a pair) in the fairing. *(Shuttleworth Collection)*

Bombs

In addition to the bomb carrier wings on the sides of the undercarriage legs, another carrier could be attached below the rear fuselage structure. Both the pilot and the occupant of the prone bomb-aiming position could release and jettison the bombs, but only the pilot was able to select and fuse them. The Lysander's full bomb load was either sixteen 20-pounders, four 120-pounders or two 250-pounders.

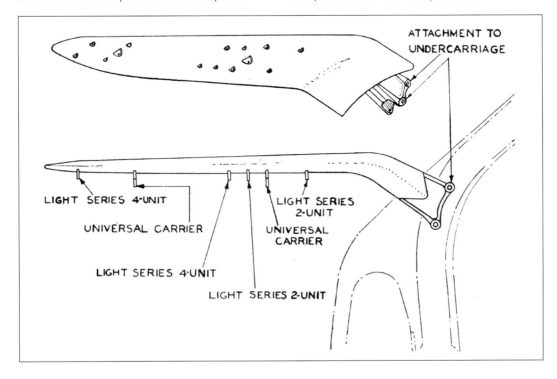

ATTACHMENT TO UNDERCARRIAGE

LIGHT SERIES 4-UNIT

UNIVERSAL CARRIER

LIGHT SERIES 4-UNIT

LIGHT SERIES 2-UNIT

UNIVERSAL CARRIER

LIGHT SERIES 2-UNIT

LEFT Bomb wing attachment detail. *(Shuttleworth Collection)*

Cameras

The Lysander was capable of carrying two cameras. One was mounted on the rear cockpit floor and operated by the pilot with a remote control and a bead sight located at the base of the control column. Doors in the fuselage fairing allowed for either vertical or oblique photography. The other camera was positioned on the leading edge of the starboard wing. The control for this camera was the gun-firing button on the pilot's control column.

Message pick-up hook

A hinged arm supported by a control cable wound on a winch with a hook on the end could be provided for picking up messages while the Lysander was flying close to the ground. Messages could be removed from the hook through a door in the underside of the fuselage fairing.

Parachute stowage

The pilot's seat was shaped to take a seat-type parachute. The parachute for the occupant of the rear cockpit was stowed in a plywood box on the port side of the fuselage.

Miscellaneous items

Other items carried on board included a chart board, a first-aid box, a fire extinguisher, a hold-all for Lewis gun spares, parachute flares and a signal pistol and cartridges in the rear cockpit, while a map case and an axe were stowed in the pilot's cockpit.

The Bristol Mercury engine

The designer

If Lysander pilots had the ingenuity of Teddy Petter and Arthur Davenport to thank for the unique attributes of the aircraft's design, they owed as much for their safety and effectiveness to the man who designed the engine that powered their propeller. This man was Roy Fedden of the Bristol Engine Company.

Like Petter, Fedden had a relatively prosperous, public school upbringing, his parents owning one of the first motor cars to be seen in the Bristol area. His fascination with this machine was enough to persuade the young man to take up an engineering apprenticeship, and by the time he had turned 21, in 1906, he had designed a car of his own. Taken on by local firm Brazil, Straker and Co., his design was developed into the successful 12/14 Shamrock of 1907. Fedden soon became responsible for all motor vehicle design and production for the company, and

RIGHT The nine-cylinder Bristol Mercury radial engine of the Shuttleworth Trust's Lysander receives attention.

with the outbreak of war in 1914 he persuaded the management to add aircraft engine repair to the company's list of services. Before long they were producing aero-engines for Rolls Royce, Renault and Curtiss under Fedden's direction.

In fact, Fedden had declined a senior position offered by Frederick Royce in favour of remaining with Brazil, Straker and Co. where, in 1915, he embarked on designing his own aircraft engine with the aid of his draughtsman, Leonard Butler. The result was two different radial engines, both of which outperformed their competitors in tests on aircraft designed by the Bristol Aeroplane Company. Unfortunately for Fedden and his colleagues, the end of the war saw an abrupt cancellation of orders for his new engines, and Cosmos Engineering – as the aviation portion of his company had become – was soon insolvent.

Rescue came in the shape of a takeover by the Bristol Aeroplane Company and, with Fedden in charge of the new engine division, he saw the larger of his two engine designs, the 400hp Bristol Jupiter, become a commercial success in the early 1920s, with worldwide sales.

As the decade wore on there was an increasing demand for more power from smaller, lighter engines. The incorporation of superchargers to boost aircraft performance at altitude, where the air is thinner, had become widespread at the time and Roy Fedden was one of the first to realise that they could be used in small measure at all times to improve an engine's overall performance. Without having to design a completely new engine block, he reused the existing Jupiter engine parts but reduced the stroke by an inch. He thus created a smaller engine that could nonetheless be boosted back to much higher power levels than had previously been achieved. The radial nine-cylinder Bristol Mercury was born, an engine that would eventually power more than 40 different types of aircraft and of which some 20,700 versions were built.

General characteristics of a radial aero-engine

A radial engine has one or more rows of cylinders arranged in a circle around the crankcase. Each row usually has an odd

PARTICULARS OF THE BRISTOL MERCURY XX ENGINE

Type:	Air-cooled radial.
Number of cylinders:	9.
Arrangement of cylinders:	Single bank.
Bore:	5.75in.
Stroke:	6.5in.
Swept volume:	1,520in^3.
Compression ratio:	6.25 to 1.
Supercharger –	
Degree of supercharge:	Moderate altitude.
Gear ratio:	9.4 to 1.
Airscrew reduction gear –	
Type:	Bevel epicyclic.
Ratio:	Approx. 572 to 1.
Direction of rotation –	
Airscrew shaft:	Left-hand.
Crankshaft:	Left-hand.
Cylinder numbering:	1, 2, 3, 4, 5, 6, 7, 8, 9, clockwise from front, number 1 vertical.
Weight (nett dry):	1,062lb.
Rated altitude:	2,500ft.
International power rating:	775/810bhp at 2,400rpm at 2,500ft at 4¼lb per square inch boost.
Maximum power rating:	835/870bhp at 2,750rpm at 4,500ft and 4¼lb per square inch boost.
Fuel type:	100 octane.
Fuel consumption –	
Max climbing conditions:	68 gallons per hour.
Economical cruising:	0.525 pint per bhp/hour.
Oil consumption:	6 to 12 pints per hour.
Main oil pressure:	Normal: 80lb per square inch. Emergency minimum: 70lb per square inch.
Inlet oil temperatures:	Minimum for opening up: 5°C. Maximum for continuous cruising: 70°C. Maximum for climbing: 80°C. Emergency maximum: 90°C.
Ignition firing order:	1, 3, 5, 7, 2, 4, 6, 8.
Number of magnetos:	Two, counter-clockwise rotation, at 1.125 times engine rotation.
Carburettor:	Master control, including automatic boost and mixture control units.
Propeller:	de Havilland three-blade two-pitch propeller of 11ft diameter and 10° pitch range.

number of cylinders, which gives a smoother operation. The piston rods of each row of cylinders drive a single-crank throw allowing, for a relatively small crankcase, which in turn ensures a favourable power-to-weight ratio. (A radial engine should not be confused with

a rotary engine whose crankshaft is fixed to the airframe and whose propeller is fixed to the engine case, so that the crankcase and cylinders rotate.)

The cylinder arrangement of a radial engine exposes much of the engine's heat-radiating surfaces to the air and cancels reciprocating forces, allowing for even cooling and smooth running. There is a tendency for the lower cylinders under the crankcase to collect oil when the engine has been unused for a time. To avoid the catastrophic effects of hydrostatic lock (when a liquid prevents the piston from completing its travel within the cylinder), this oil has to be cleared from the cylinders before the engine is started.

Although the large frontal area of an aircraft fitted with a radial engine reduces its

LEFT The de Havilland three-blade variable-pitch propeller with spinner, oil cooler air intakes and cowling mounting struts (behind).

aerodynamic efficiency, its bulk does provide some protection from bullets for the pilot of a military aeroplane. The air-cooled system also means that with no vulnerable radiator, a radial engine is less susceptible to battle damage than one cooled by water.

The Lysander engines

The two 1936 prototype Lysanders were fitted with a Bristol Mercury IX, which, despite what its Roman numeral suggests, was the 19th version of the engine since the Mercury I was built in 1926. It was fully supercharged and gave 840hp at 14,000ft at 2,750rpm. The next 188 Mk I Lysanders were powered by the Bristol Mercury XII, which was medium supercharged and gave 890hp at 6,000ft at 2,750rpm. This rating at a lower altitude was considered to be better suited to the Lysander's army cooperation work and so was chosen for the first production run.

However, Westland had also run tests using a different engine in the two prototype Lysanders, namely the Bristol Perseus. This engine was a variation from the Mercury, developed by Roy Fedden, using sleeve rather than poppet valves, which improved the performance by allowing a greater capacity for intake and exhaust expulsion to and from the cylinders. The Mk II Lysanders (of which 441 were built) were subsequently fitted with the Perseus XII engine, a medium supercharged version giving 905hp at 6,500ft at 2,750rpm.

The need to meet the urgent demand for fighters and bombers to defend Britain's shores after the fall of France in 1940 meant a standardisation in engine building programmes. Westland's had to revert to a Mercury poppet valve engine, this one designated the Mercury XX. All Lysanders fitted with this engine were known as Mk IIIs, of which more than 800 were built. A modification to the Mercury XX whereby a white metal crankshaft bearing was introduced in 1941 in place of a floating one changed the otherwise identical engine's designation to the Mercury 30.

RIGHT Detachable engine cowling panels.

PARTICULARS OF THE BRISTOL PERSEUS ENGINE

General characteristics

Type:	Nine-cylinder single-row supercharged air-cooled radial engine.
Bore:	5.75in (146mm).
Stroke:	6.5in (165mm).
Displacement:	1,520in^3 (24.9l).
Length:	49in (1,245mm).
Diameter:	55.3in (1,405mm).
Dry weight:	1,025lb (465kg).

Components

Valve train:	Sleeve valve.
Supercharger:	Single-speed centrifugal type supercharger.
Fuel system:	Claudel-Hobson carburettor.
Fuel type:	87 octane petrol.
Cooling system:	Air-cooled.
Reduction gear:	0.5:1 turning a de Havilland variable-pitch propeller.

Performance

Power output:	830hp (619kW) at 2,650rpm for take-off, 905hp (675kW) at 2,750rpm at 6,500ft (1,980m).
Specific power:	0.59hp/in^3 (26.75kW/l).
Compression ratio:	6.75:1.
Specific fuel consumption:	0.43lb/(hp·h) (261g/(kW·h)).
Oil consumption:	0.28oz/(hp·h) (11g/(kW·h)).
Power-to-weight ratio:	0.88hp/lb (1.45kW/kg).

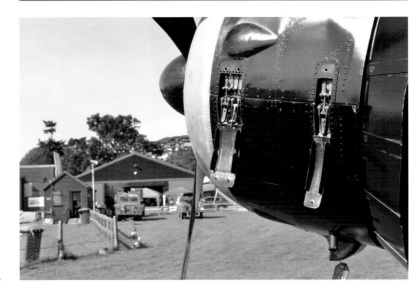

Chapter Four

Cloak-and-dagger operations

The Lysander found its true métier in providing a night-time shuttle service in and out of occupied France, carrying agents of the Secret Intelligence Service and the Special Operations Executive between October 1940 and August 1944. Such was the navigational skill of the pilots of 161 (Special Duties) Squadron that only six of them lost their lives in more than 200 missions flown.

OPPOSITE **The Shuttleworth Lysander V9367 painted overall in black and fitted with an under-slung long-range fuel tank to represent a Special Duties Lysander of No 161 Squadron at Tempsford.** *(PRM Aviation Collection)*

A dumpy black aeroplane, barely visible in the fading autumn moonlight, but highly audible, circles a desolate patch of French farmland at a height of about 300ft. The silhouette of its pilot's rounded head can just be seen through the cockpit glass, craning towards the ground, scouring the terrain. The plane makes another circuit, then another. Lights begin to appear in the windows of one or two of the neighbouring farmhouses – it has been overhead now for more than 15 minutes. Finally its wings level out, the throttle opens, and it begins a climb towards the north. Almost immediately, the engine revs fall again and the plane banks sharply to the right. Nearly a mile from where it had been circling, a light on the ground is flashing a regular dash–dash–dot – the letter 'G'.

There are two short bursts on the throttle from the aircraft, now making straight for the light, and, in response, the light switches to a steady beam; then two more lights appear, completing a flare path. After one circuit of what appears to be a very small grass field with a road and a line of tall trees at the windward end, the pilot makes his approach, dropping almost vertically from the sky. The plane thumps down on to the turf just to the right of the first torch, bounces forward drunkenly over the heavily pitted surface and halts abruptly after scarcely 50yd. With its propeller still tearing at the night air, the aircraft turns and taxis back to the marker light furthest from the line of trees. In an instant, one man has clambered out of the rear cockpit and another is installed, strapping himself into his harness as the revs pick up.

The engine is now screaming as if in panic as the pilot tries to gather speed on the rough terrain. Each bump checks the acceleration and the trees at the end of the field are now only 100yd away. The wheel hits yet another hummock, but this one throws the plane into the air. It climbs at an improbable angle but the trees seem to have grown in height. Then there is a blinding flash and the aeroplane wobbles for a second in its trajectory. But its engine roars on and, with the undercarriage thrashing through the treetops, heaves itself clear. As the plane climbs northwards and disappears into the blackness, hanging limply from a nearby pole a severed high-tension electricity cable and a finer telephone wire snake among the fresh leaves and broken twigs that now litter the field beneath the trees.

An hour and a half later, the same aeroplane is 14,000ft above the north coast of France. Its sedate progress is suddenly broken as it makes a tight diving turn to the left. Passing about 300ft overhead are two German night-fighters on patrol, their green starboard navigation lights clearly visible. As they reach the end of their patrol line, they turn in neat formation through 180° and retrace their original route. The unlit black aeroplane, which had initially headed evasively back into France, has turned now once more towards the Channel as it makes a steep dive towards the water, pulling out when just a few feet above the waves. Only when

BELOW One of the first Lysander Mk IIIAs to be fitted with a long-range fuel tank. *(RAF Museum)*

the pilot is certain he has remained undetected does he pull up to 2,000ft and head for home.

Home is not welcoming. A low-lying fog covers the runway, but the approach lights are just visible on the ends of their poles above it. The plane sinks into the fog, nose high, feeling for the ground, so the tail wheel touches the tarmac first. It is safely down. A jeep appears out of the gloom and escorts the aircraft to a safe parking place. When the pilot descends stiffly from his cockpit – he has been in the air for five hours and forty minutes – he peers at the undercarriage, disentangles a length of telephone wire and puts it in his pocket to keep as a souvenir.

The aircraft in this first clandestine operation of No 138 Special Duties Squadron, on the night of 4 September 1941, was a Westland Lysander Mk III SCW, or a 'Lizzie', as they were fondly nicknamed. The pilot, Flight Lieutenant John Nesbitt-Dufort, had skilfully demonstrated in his very first trip just how well suited the Lysander was to the business of ferrying secret service agents in and out of France during the Occupation. On this occasion, its ability to land and take off in a confined space was tested to an unreasonable extreme. The incoming agent and his assistant had been delayed in leaving their hotel by a police inspection of all the guests' papers. When still a mile from the pre-selected landing field, they could hear the Lysander circling and guessed that it was unlikely to stay around long enough for them to get to the field on their bicycles. They therefore chose the nearest likely field and began their signalling. No one had spotted the power lines in the darkness.

As we have already seen in earlier chapters, the Lysander had been built originally to operate mainly by day as part of a team over a battlefield, seeking out enemy artillery and strongholds and generally providing assistance to their army colleagues on the ground. The events of early summer 1940 were to expose the aircraft's vulnerability in such a role, which, in any case, proved virtually unworkable in the circumstances of Hitler's *Blitzkrieg*. It was thus a fortunate coincidence when the RAF discovered that they possessed in the Lysander a perfect vehicle to carry out the very different clandestine task that, since the fall of France, they were increasingly

asked to perform by the Secret Intelligence Service and the Special Operations Executive.

The practice of placing agents behind enemy lines and of retrieving them by air was not an entirely new one. The flamboyant French aviator, Jules Védrines, winner of many early international air races, is renowned for his daring flights in a small monoplane across the German defences during the First World War, to land and pick up intelligence agents. The first such operation by the British was attempted by a Captain Thomas Mulcahy Morgan in September 1915, but both he and his clandestine passenger were badly injured after their BE 2c crashed on landing, and they were both captured. Other more successful missions were completed in the ensuing weeks and months.

From its Royal Flying Corps roots, the RAF therefore had some idea of what was required and, in September 1940, established No 419 Flight, which comprised three Lysanders and two Whitley twin-engine bombers adapted for parachuting purposes. Originally based at North Weald near Epping in Essex, the flight was moved, following a damaging German bombing raid, to Stradishall in Suffolk only a month after its formation.

One of its first 'customers' was the SIS agent Phillip Schneidau, a man raised in Paris of two British parents, who played international hockey for France before choosing British nationality at the age of 21. His mission in France was to last ten days. The plan was for him to be dropped by parachute from a Whitley and recovered at the end by the squadron's commander, Flight Lieutenant Wally Farley, who would land a Lysander on a prearranged field to the south of Fontainebleau. The two men had designed the inverted 'L'-shaped pattern of lights – a device that never needed improvement throughout the war – on a tablecloth at Oddenino's restaurant in Regent Street.

Thick cloud and heavy rain prevented Farley from setting off from Tangmere on the predetermined night of the pickup, but the following evening, 19 October 1940, he left in equally poor weather as he was concerned that Schneidau would believe he had been abandoned. Fortunately the skies cleared over France, but not before the radio in the rear cockpit had been put out of action by the rain

– Farley had left the sliding roof open to make it easier for Schneidau to clamber in. The pickup went without a hitch, Schneidau using the fixed ladder he had invented for rapid embarkation. Someone on the ground had spotted them, however, because shortly after take-off a bullet shot through the bottom of the fuselage, passed between the pilot's legs and hammered into the compass.

Back over the French coast the weather worsened, and almost immediately – with no view of the ground, no compass and no radio – they became utterly lost. Although he realised his passenger was freezing in the open cockpit behind him, Farley felt his only option was to fly on until they could see something. They flew on for several hours, all the time fearing that the strong south-westerly wind had carried them over Belgium, Holland or even Germany. With all fuel spent and dawn breaking, they finally saw a coastline and Farley, gliding now, brought the Lysander down at the top of some high cliffs. The aircraft lost both wings on touching down thanks to poles that had been erected to prevent such landings, but both occupants were unhurt. Still not knowing whether they were on home or enemy territory, Farley decided he would go to find help and told Schneidau to strip naked and be ready to throw his incriminating civilian clothes over the cliff if he returned with a German escort. When he did eventually come back, accompanied by two armed and uniformed men, he greeted his shivering friend: 'I can't understand a word they are saying, but it appears we are in Scotland – somewhere near Oban.'

No further calls for clandestine night landings were made on the Lysanders of the renumbered 1419 Flight for the next six months. Then, in April 1941, Flying Officer Gordon Scotter successfully retrieved an agent from a field north of Châteauroux, in spite of an encounter with night-fighters fitted with searchlights and a narrow escape from Vichy police on the ground. The following month he flew to Fontainebleau to collect Phillip Schneidau, who had returned to France to set up an intelligence ring in Paris. The operation proved a far smoother affair than Schneidau's first return to Britain.

Demand now began to grow for special duties air operations, and the RAF expanded its facility accordingly. First, in August, the flight took on squadron status, No 138, and moved to Newmarket, using the heath beside the racecourse as its runway. By December 1941, after four more Lysander operations – including John Nesbitt-Dufort's close encounter with a power cable – the squadron comprised 18 aircraft. In February of the following year a second special duties squadron was formed, No 161, which, from its eventual home of RAF Tempsford near Sandy in Bedfordshire, would bear responsibility for all the Lysander pickups in France until the end of the war.

By the end of 1941 the Lysander pilots had begun to perfect their routines both in solo navigation by moonlight and in reducing the time spent on enemy soil to a minimum. All the Lysanders in the squadron had been specially adapted for their task, which, as well as Schneidau's ladder, included an additional torpedo-shaped 150-gallon fuel tank slung beneath the forward fuselage to give them the range required to get deep into France and back. The Mk III SCW, as it was known, carried no armaments, to reduce its overall weight so that it could take as many passengers and their luggage as possible. The limit was normally two people sharing the passenger seat, but if a third had to be carried they would lie on the floor, and when (very rarely) a fourth was carried they would have to sit on the cockpit shelf. The special duties Lysanders sported an all-black colour scheme for night-time camouflage. The paint pattern was later modified, with the underside remaining matt black while the tops of the wings and fuselage reverted to dark green and pale grey, a better camouflage

BELOW Special duties Lysander Mk III R9125 of No 161 Squadron with the extra fuel tank slung underneath the fuselage and the fixed port-side rear cockpit ladder. This aircraft is now on display at the RAF Museum, Hendon. It starred in the film *Now It Can Be Told*, which was premiered in February 1947 and told something of the wartime Special Duties Operations. *(Bertram family)*

against night-fighters approaching from above in moonlight.

The pilots chosen to fly the Lysander missions had to be utterly self-reliant by nature. Even the training for the job was a do-it-yourself process. The minimum qualification was 250 hours of night-flying experience, and an ability to speak French was desirable if not essential. So too, albeit unstated, was an acceptance of very adverse odds against surviving any operation. One man, Hugh Verity, recruited into No 161 Squadron in November 1942, described his training in his definitive post-war account of the Lysanders' special duties, *We Landed by Moonlight*:

'The training – which I was largely left to work out for myself – had to turn me into a competent special duties Lysander pilot in about a month. I had to be able to fly the aeroplane, to fly it by night, to land it on a ridiculous little flare path and to navigate it by moonlight to any field in France.

'I took stock of the situation. I had done about 850 hours, of which about 250 were by night. I had been trained as a navigator as well as a pilot, but I had not done very much pilot-navigation, and none of that had been at night. The others showed me how they prepared their route maps and worked out their flight plans, but I knew I needed a lot of practice.'

Before his first flight, Verity sat in a Lysander cockpit with the 20-page pilot's notes and taught himself how to locate all the controls by touch alone. He also learnt all the drills, checks and limits by heart. After that, he was ready to take the plane up. Strapping himself into his seat and sliding the cockpit canopy shut, he primed the engine and started up. Waiting for the oil temperature to rise to 5°C, he tested the flying controls and brake pressure. Then, against the brakes and the chocks, he opened up to 1,800rpm and changed the pitch of the propeller to coarse. Noting the large drop in revs, he returned to the fine-pitch position and throttled back. Now, almost ready to go, he checked that

ABOVE Mk IIIA Lysanders in the process of being fitted with long-range fuel tanks at Westland's. (AgustaWestland)

BELOW Mk IIIA Lysander (T1771) with long-range additional fuel tank on Westland's airstrip. (AgustaWestland)

the tail actuating wheel was set for take-off, that the fuel mixture control was at 'normal' and that the gills were open to increase airflow over the engine. Finally, with chocks removed, he taxied on to the runway, eased the throttle fully open and, travelling at a speed of 80mph, pulled the stick back and climbed away.

The next stage of his training was to practise the landing and take-off routines repeatedly in daylight on a grassy field at Somersham in Cambridgeshire, some 30 miles from Tempsford, using yellow flags in place of torches. Then he tested himself landing at night and on one occasion accomplished eight landings in a space of 40 minutes. In barely a week he had become completely at ease with bringing a Lysander down in darkness with the aid of three pocket torches marking a landing site just 150yd long.

Much of his earlier flying with the RAF had been done with the luxury of a navigator, so as part of his training he took himself on extended flights over England by both day and night to improve his pathfinding ability. Apart from one panic-inducing moment during a night flight when he thought for a while that he had become completely lost and would have to face the ignominy of radioing for his position, he generally kept his bearings, including during a three-hour, non-stop round trip between Tempsford and Exeter.

The last part of Verity's initiation came when he went to join the other Lysander pilots of the squadron who had moved to their advance base at Tangmere for the moon-period operations. To prove his ability in finding an exact position over enemy territory, he was given a pinpoint to fly to, south of Saumur, on the Loire. He was shown how to make his way through a corridor free of flak and how to cut strips out of 1:500,000 maps, showing the track he was to follow plus about 50 miles on either side for easy reckoning. The corridor did not prove to be flak-free, but he watched the tracers just miss him as he carried on, following his course with little difficulty. When he reached the given position, he was astonished to see a brilliantly lit rectangle, which he took to be some kind of prison camp. On his safe return to Tangmere he reported this strange sight amid all the blacked-out darkness and was immediately told he had passed the final test, as it proved he had actually been to where he was meant to go. The camp was a German prison for gypsies, its perimeter fence floodlit in case of escape attempts.

If the success of the Lysander missions depended on the exceptional skills of the pilots and the diligence of the squadron engineers, they could have accomplished little without a practised reception party in France. This was achieved by getting prospective agents and pilots together for training both at Tempsford and at Somersham for practical work. The agents, all dressed as British army officers, were taught how to set up a flare path into the wind, with the man in charge and the waiting passengers posted nearest to lamp 'A', the touchdown point. Lamp 'B' should be positioned 150m further upwind, with lamp 'C' 50m to the right of it, completing the shorter length of the inverted 'L'. The flare path needed to begin at least 100m from the nearest hedge on a clear, firm, level strip of ground, a good 600m from hedge to hedge. There could be no trees of any height in the way of the approach or take-off zones, and any cart tracks needed to be well away from the landing area. Short-grazed grass was the ideal surface but a firm field of stubble would do. Mud had to be avoided at all costs.

During part of the week-long course, agents would be driven around the local countryside and asked to point out to the pilots fields which they believed fitted the required specification. Back in the classroom they would learn how to draft descriptions of their chosen landing sites for the wireless messages sent back from France. This was important, not only for the Lysander pilots themselves but for the daytime missions that would be sent in advance to take high-altitude photographs of the proposed sites for approval by the RAF.

The landing routine itself began with the agent in charge flashing the predetermined signal letter on lamp 'A'. Once the Lysander had acknowledged this, the agent or his assistant, if he had one, would light the other two lamps. They were taught how to lash these three torches to sticks, pointing downwind and slightly upwards. They would then rehearse a three-minute turnaround on the ground whereby the last outbound passenger would pass down his own luggage and load that of those leaving France before he left the aircraft; then the new passengers would clamber aboard and, with the canopy slid shut, the pilot, on receiving a thumbs-up from the man in charge on the ground, would open up the throttle and pull away.

Lysanders were used in 204 separate operations over France between October 1940 and August 1944 and were unarguably the principal instrument in the task of ferrying men and women in and out of occupied

France. There was, however, another aircraft flown by No 161 Squadron for the same purpose that should not be overlooked. This was the American-built Lockheed Hudson, a military conversion of a commercial airliner, the Lockheed 14 Super Electra, perhaps most famous for conveying Neville Chamberlain to and from Germany during his ill-fated pre-war shuttle diplomacy with Hitler. The main reason the squadron had a Hudson at its disposal appears to be that its first commanding officer, Wing Commander E.H. ('Mouse') Fielden, who had just come from the job of pilot to the King, had brought the plane with him from the King's Flight.

A low-wing monoplane with twin Cyclone radial engines, the Hudson was recognisable particularly by its long tailplane with twin pear-shaped fins and rudders near the rounded ends. The nose of the plane was fitted with Perspex windows for the bomb aimer, and a gunner's turret projected from the top of the rear fuselage. Most of this reconnaissance bomber's wartime service was spent over the Atlantic, providing protection to convoys against submarines.

For the clandestine purposes of No 161 Squadron, the Hudson was a far less subtle instrument than the Lysander. It was about

BELOW The twin-engine Lockheed Hudson was the other aircraft used by No 161 Squadron for moonlit landings in France. It came in to land 10kts faster than the Lysander and needed a flare path of 350m in a field no shorter than 1,000m. This is Hudson Mk I, N7221 'MA-P', making a low pass over the runway at Tempsford. In the background can be seen a Short Stirling and a handful of Handley Page Halifaxes parked at dispersals. These larger aircraft types were also used by the Tempsford squadrons for special duties operations dropping agents and supplies. (IWM HU60553)

three times heavier and came in to land a good ten knots faster, needing a flare path of 350m in a field no shorter than 1,000m. It was therefore a considerable headache for agents in France to find suitable landing sites and required many helpers, including armed guards at the perimeters, as the larger planes attracted far more attention than the agile Lysander. The advantage was the plane's greater range and, above all, its capacity, as it could take up to ten passengers and their luggage. As the war progressed and the intelligence and SOE networks grew, increasing numbers had to be flown in and out of France, and it was therefore preferable to use one Hudson rather than three or even four Lysanders on a single operation. Another considerable advantage to the pilot of a Hudson was that there was space for a navigator on board. In all, the Hudson was used in 39 missions to deliver and collect agents.

The men who flew the Lysanders ('A' Flight) of No 161 Squadron were a select few. At any given time they would number no more than five, and throughout the years between October 1940 and August 1944, when the moonlit operations were run from Tangmere, only 35 pilots were involved in total. It meant, of course, that they were a close-knit team, living at close quarters, particularly during the fortnightly operational periods at Tangmere when the moon was at its fullest. They would constantly learn from one another's experiences, both good and bad. Each must have felt a sense of utter loneliness every time they set off into the night to pick their way across dark and hostile terrain towards their unmarked target. Even when an operation involved two or three

Lysanders at a time, they could not follow a leader but had to find their way on their own.

Hugh Verity, who commanded the Lysander flight for the whole of 1943, its busiest year, had flown 36 missions in that time. He later wrote:

'The end of my tour of operations released the tension on the spring which I had kept more tightly wound up than I had realised. I suddenly collapsed and was good for nothing but staying in bed for the best part of a week. A medical check-up revealed that I was totally exhausted. From 6 to 16 November we laid on operations on eight nights out of eleven. I had myself flown on five of these nights and been responsible until pilots were safely landed and debriefed on all eight. Apart from the nervous tension – which one did not notice at the time – this routine left us all very short of ordinary sleep.'

It was a strange way to fight a war. Apart from the pistol each pilot carried for self-defence, there was no means of combat. Half of every month was spent completely free from danger in rural Bedfordshire, training agents and visiting home and loved ones while waiting for the next moon period. The other half, by contrast, was a fortnight of intense anticipation by day followed by a night of either high adventure or frustrating anticlimax when bad weather intervened.

Life on the ground at Tangmere was spent mainly at what was known as 'The Cottage'. Standing opposite the main gates of the RAF station behind a tall hedge, it was a 17th-century dwelling which had been extended considerably over the years. Apart from its kitchen, where the establishment's two flight sergeant security minders doubled as cooks, preparing mixed grills and sumptuous breakfasts for returning

pilots and agents, there were two other rooms downstairs. One was for dining and the other was the operations and crew room. In it was a large map of France, with the areas defended by flak marked in red. As well as a table and a map chest, an assortment of armchairs was arranged around the coal fire. The only real clue to the clandestine role of the cottage's inhabitants was a green 'scrambler' phone positioned next to the standard black one.

Upstairs there were some six bedrooms, all with as many beds as there was space for. It was not only the pilots these had to accommodate before and after operations, but SOE agents and all other passengers except those chaperoned by the SIS, who were lodged at Bignor Manor, a farmhouse just north of the Downs. Bignor Manor was the house of an SIS conducting officer, Major Tony Bertram, and his wife Barbara. Throughout the years of the special duties flights from Tangmere, Barbara Bertram had the task of providing board and lodging for French intelligence agents while they waited for suitable weather for their outward flight or after they had been brought back from France.

The exuberance of the young pilots, most in their early 20s, occasionally bubbled over beyond the confines of The Cottage. They would sometimes take their planes up on days of cancelled operations and swoop low over Bignor Manor, terrifying both Barbara Bertram

LEFT Interior of Bignor Manor photographed during the war. The dart board was mounted for the entertainment of agents during their stay at Bignor. The panel behind it concealed a store of espionage supplies and equipment, which included maps printed on silk, fountain pens that released tear gas, pistols and cyanide pills. *(Bertram family)*

LEFT Barbara and Tony Bertram of Bignor Manor, where French agents of the Secret Intelligence Service were clandestinely housed before and after their passage by Lysander in and out of occupied France. *(Bertram family)*

and her goat, Caroline. At one stage an order appeared in the flight headquarters forbidding any low flying over Bignor until Caroline was delivered of the kid she was expecting. Caroline, a celebrity among both agents and pilots, was later immortalised when her name was used for one of the pickup operations. All week prior to the operation, the BBC had solemnly announced news of Caroline: 'Caroline has a new hat.' 'Caroline is well.' 'Caroline went for a walk. Finally there came: 'Caroline has a blue dress' – blue being the associated word telling the French landing party that the mission was on for that night.

The pilots who flew the Lysander missions later in the war owed much to two of the pioneers of special duties pickups, John ('Whippy') Nesbitt-Dufort, DSO, Croix de Guerre, and Alan ('Sticky') Murphy, DSO, DFC, Croix de Guerre. These two skilful aviators and impressive individuals were anything but the run-of-the-mill caricatures of wartime RAF pilot officers suggested by their schoolboy nicknames and mustachioed looks. Both brought back valuable lessons to the squadron after narrow escapes on enemy soil, and one ultimately owed his deliverance from a Gestapo manhunt to the other.

John Nesbitt-Dufort, born in 1912, was brought up in the Home Counties by his grandmother and uncles and aunts after his French father was killed on the Western Front in 1914 and his English mother died a few years later. Passionate about aeroplanes and engines from a very early age, he was accepted as an RAF trainee pilot officer at the earliest permissible age of 17½. Showing above-average aptitude on gaining his wings, he spent his short commission with a fighter squadron, then as an instructor. When war broke out, he had left the RAF and was working with de Havilland, teaching young men destined for military duty to fly Tiger Moths. He soon joined up again and, after a spell of training bomber pilots, then piloting a night-fighter, he was recruited for special duties with No 138 Squadron.

He flew five missions during his tour of duty with them between September 1941 and March 1942. The first, the nearly disastrous encounter with a French power cable, convinced his superiors to step up the training for agents in charge of pickups in the selection of appropriate landing sites. The second, to a field west of Soissons, near Reims, went without a serious hitch, while the third, to around the same region of France, had to be abandoned when mist obscured the agents' landing lights. Nesbitt-Dufort returned the following night, however, and brought home one of the SIS's star Polish agents, Roman Garby-Czerniawski, who was head of the Paris-based network *Interallié*. The weather, especially in winter, presented as much danger to the Lysander operations as any German firepower and, when Nesbitt-Dufort set off on his fifth mission in January 1942 it all but got the better of him and his passengers.

Apart from some mercifully inaccurate flak over the French coast, the outward journey and landing in a field near Issoudun went according to plan thanks to clear moonlight over central France. Roger Mitchell, a French agent recruited by General de Gaulle's head of intelligence in London, André Dewavrin, alias Passy, to organise pickups in France, was now on his way back to England with an important package. He had done his job of field selection well. In a matter of minutes, he and his companion, Maurice Duclos, were crammed into the Lysander's rear cockpit and watching the dark French countryside shrinking beneath them. Duclos, Passy's very first agent, had been on the run in France since the previous August, when his Paris-based network had been betrayed by the Luxembourger double agent André Folmer. Although he had narrowly avoided capture, many of his network were caught and eventually shot, while his doting older sister and her niece, with whom he lived, were tortured by the Gestapo and sent to a concentration camp.

The flight back over France at about 7,000ft was uneventful until, 80 miles south of the French coast, the air started to become turbulent. 'Suddenly I saw it,' John Nesbitt-Dufort recalls in his book, *Black Lysander*:

'It must have formed up rapidly along the north French coast during the last three hours. "It" was the most wicked-looking and well-defined active cold front I had ever seen. It extended right across my track to the east and west as far as the eye could see and the top of that boiling mass of cumulonimbus clouds, seething upwards like the heavy smoke of some gigantic oil fire, must have risen to well over 30,000ft – way above the maximum altitude of the Lizzie. From the base of that horror, which was only about 600ft above the ground, torrential rain fell, while lightning played continually in its black depths.'

Seeing that there was no way round either to the west or to the east, Nesbitt-Dufort first opted to descend to 1,000ft and attempt to fly under the mass of cloud. He soon realised this was a mistake; in the pitch darkness, the rain was forcing his plane ever lower to the ground and his windscreen was white with ice. He made an about turn and emerged again in the clear air, thoroughly shaken up. His next attempt was to fly through the middle of the cloud at about 10,000ft, relying entirely on his instruments to see him through. Almost immediately the Lysander began to be tossed around, as he put it, 'like a leaf in a whirlwind'. Blinded by the continual lightning, his compass unreliable from the amount of static and his airspeed indicator iced up and useless, Nesbitt-Dufort fought on at his controls using all the power he could squeeze out of the engine. But the aircraft was losing height. Opening the cockpit window, he thrust his gloved hand into the slipstream and when he brought it back

found it petrified in a clear coating of ice. The same would be happening on all the exterior surfaces of the Lysander, the wings unable to provide the lift needed for the extra weight.

Then the engine, its carburettor choking with ice, began to splutter and, down to 7,000ft, the aircraft was tumbling, virtually out of control. Nesbitt-Dufort got on the intercom to his two passengers – whom he had tried unsuccessfully to rouse earlier in the flight – and told them, in no uncertain terms, that they should prepare to bail out. There was no reply from them and he soon realised to his horror that they had failed to don their helmets for the flight so were unable to receive the command. They had, in fact, also failed to fit their parachutes, but with no visual communication between a Lysander pilot and his passengers Nesbitt-Dufort would not have known this. All he did know was that if his 'Joes' were sitting tight, he would have to do the same.

At 5,000ft he pointed the nose downwards in an attempt to gain speed to have enough control to turn the plane through 180°, in a desperate attempt to retreat from the storm. At any moment he expected the wings to come off in the turbulence but, to his astonished relief, with the altimeter reading 900ft, he broke

BELOW John Nesbitt-Dufort's abandoned Lysander is inspected by officials after he was forced to land in central France after encountering nearly fatal weather conditions on a return trip to England with two agents aboard in January 1942. The plane hit a ditch on landing but the pilot and passengers escaped capture and made it back to Britain a few weeks later.
(Bertram family)

cloud. The engine, although still extremely weak at first, picked up enough for him to fly on for an hour until, very short of fuel, he put down in a field. The field, unfortunately, had an unseen ditch running across it which caught the Lysander's undercarriage, tipping it on to the propeller and throwing pilot and passengers violently forward. Much later in his life an X-ray revealed scars from a triple whiplash fracture, but at the time he assumed that he had simply cricked his neck.

Although he knew he must have landed somewhere in central France, Nesbitt-Dufort had no idea where. As for his passengers, they were asking where the car was to take them to London and expressed exasperated disappointment when told where they had fetched up. It took some explaining by their pilot to convince them how fortunate they were to still be breathing. They would later learn just how fortunate; that same night, 36 British bombers failed to return from a mission, nearly all their losses due to the effect of icing in the storm.

Orders were to destroy an abandoned plane in France but, despite three attempts, it would not catch fire, mainly because all the fuel had been used up. The next priority was to put distance between themselves and the Lysander and discover where they were. They made off across muddy fields and through undergrowth in the darkness and freezing rain that had now reached them, until they came upon a road and a signpost on which they could just make out the words St Florent. The three men crouched in a hedge while Nesbitt-Dufort pulled his RAF-issue survival kit from his hip pocket. Among its contents of Benzedrine, a compass, matches, a water purifying kit, chocolate and Horlicks tablets, he was looking for a tissue-paper map of France. By the light of Mitchell's torch, he fumbled with its folds until, spread out before them, they found themselves peering at a detailed map of Germany. There was also some German currency enclosed. After a moment's silence, Mitchell and Nesbitt-Dufort could only laugh at this administrative howler. Duclos, though, was far from amused and eyed the Englishman with profound suspicion. However, Duclos believed he now knew roughly where they were: about a 20-mile walk from Issoudun,

the town close to which they had taken off several hours earlier.

History will relate that, in spite of this seemingly impossible predicament, the three men did eventually make it back to England. It took more than a month for word to be got back that they were still alive and had not been captured by the Germans, who had been hunting them down ever since the abandoned Lysander had been discovered. In fact they were sheltered by a local railwayman and his family until Duclos was able to organise false papers to be made for Nesbitt-Dufort and a landing strip could be identified for their exfiltration. The RAF had decided to make the unprecedented move of sending a twin-engine plane, powerful enough to carry the three men plus a Polish general, also on the run, who would join them on the night they were due to go.

A disused airfield close to Issoudun had been identified by Mitchell, photographed by RAF air reconnaissance and okayed by No 161 Squadron as suitable for a night landing by an Avro Anson. Finally, on the evening of 1 March, the eagerly anticipated coded BBC message came through and the four men made the arduous journey on foot to the airfield. Nesbitt-Dufort was very concerned, when they got there, that the grass field was barely firm enough to take the weight of the 3½-ton aircraft. The plane eventually came in at 12:30am and made a good landing, but with all the men and luggage on board the wheels stuck in the mud when the pilot opened the throttles for take-off. Nesbitt-Dufort knew what to do, however, and shouted to his fellow passengers to copy him and bounce up and down. The ploy worked and the Anson began to roll forward and then accelerate.

Once in the air, Nesbitt-Dufort went forward to find out which pilot had pioneered this daring landing in such an unconventional aircraft and was delighted to find his close colleague 'Sticky' Murphy at the controls. He was greeted with the words: 'John, you old bastard! You stink like the Paris Metro. Get the ruddy undercart up, will you?'

On hearing that Nesbitt-Dufort had survived the dreaded report of 'missing, believed killed on operations', Murphy had volunteered to fly the mission. The flight touched down at

Tangmere three hours later without further incident, blazing a trail of encouragement for the later twin-engine pickups using Hudsons. Four very happy and relieved passengers disembarked from the plane and were quickly immersed in the customary celebratory hospitality at The Cottage.

They could have been forgiven for not thinking of it at the time, but they would later ruefully reflect that, contained in the package that they would have delivered five weeks earlier, but for their mishap, was intelligence that the battle cruisers *Scharnhorst* and *Gneisenau* were about to leave Brest for a dash up the Channel. By the time the package was finally opened and deciphered the two ships had already, between 11 and 13 February, slipped through the Royal Navy's hands and were moored safely in German waters.

After his safe return to Tangmere, the authorities decided that John Nesbitt-Dufort should be moved from special duties flying. This was no reflection of his conduct, for which he had already been awarded the Distinguished Service Order, but rather because they felt that he knew too much about both the SIS and SOE circuits and their agents' identities in France to risk his capture and torture if things went wrong again over France. The mantle of most experienced pickup pilot was therefore passed to his friend and saviour, Squadron Leader 'Sticky' Murphy.

Murphy, from all accounts, was a cheerful, athletic extrovert whose limpid drawl reminded his fellow officers of the film actor Leslie Howard. His very first Lysander mission, on the night of 8 December 1941, could easily have been his last. He was to pick up an SOE agent from a disued airfield near the southern Belgian town of Neufchateau, but when he arrived over the airfield the familiar 'L' of lights was visible but the signal being flashed was not the agreed Morse code letter. Wanting to believe that the agent had simply made a mistake or was even in some kind of distress, Murphy decided to go ahead with the landing. Seconds before touching down, his landing light showed a deep depression in the ground ahead so he opened the throttle and flew round again. This time he chose to land a considerable distance from the flare path and sat waiting with his engine running and his pistol at the ready.

Suddenly out of the darkness came what seemed to be an explosion accompanied by a series of bright flashes. He was being fired at by an advancing company of German soldiers. Instinctively, he thrust the throttle lever forward and the Lysander was airborne again after a run-up of less than 40yd. Murphy had been hit by a bullet in the neck and, after he had gained some height and set a course for Tangmere, he pulled out a silk stocking that belonged to his wife and which he always carried as a talisman and wound it round his neck to reduce the bleeding. By the time he could call the tower at Tangmere, his voice had become drowsy from loss of blood. His course had also become erratic but thanks to the control tower's arduous efforts to keep him awake by reciting the most obscene limericks they could remember, he made it home. The Lysander was found to be peppered with some 30 bullet holes.

Back in Belgium, Captain Jean Cassart – the agent Murphy had been sent to collect – was also nursing a bullet wound, but in the arm. He, his radio operator and another helper had been surprised by the German soldiers just as they were about to switch on the flare-path lights. All three had managed to escape into the darkness amid a volley of German bullets. Cassart, hidden beneath the wall of Neufchateau cemetery, willed the Lysander pilot not to land as he watched the Germans light the three torches.

In spite of his eventual capture and incarceration in Germany, Cassart made a miraculous escape while being tried in a Berlin courtroom, and eventually made it back to England and survived the war. 'Sticky' Murphy was sadly not so fortunate. He recovered from his neck wound and went on to fly five more wholly successful special duties missions. These included one that airlifted Gilbert Renault from a snow-covered field near St Saëns, between Dieppe and Rouen in the occupied zone, and the Anson pickup of the following March. He was posted elsewhere in June 1942 and, having reached the rank of wing commander at the age of 27, his luck finally failed him when piloting a Mosquito on bomber support in December 1944. His plane was hit by flak over the Netherlands and crashed near Zwolle, killing himself and his navigator.

Guy Lockhart, having risen meteorically from the rank of flight sergeant to that of squadron leader in less than three years, succeeded 'Sticky' Murphy as commander of the Lysander special duties flight in June 1942. By then he had already completed four pickup missions from Tangmere and had previously served with distinction as a Spitfire pilot. He had had more than the fleeting acquaintance with occupied France enjoyed by most Lysander pilots, having been shot down in his Spitfire the previous July, some 20 miles inland from Boulogne. Like Nesbitt-Dufort, he experienced the hospitality and bravery of those working under cover for the Allied cause, being spirited first to Marseilles in the free zone, then on to the Pyrenean border where he was led across the mountains into Spain with a party of other fugitive British airmen. Lockhart was arrested in Spain and spent some weeks in the Nationalist concentration camp at Miranda del Ebro before his release and repatriation in October 1941.

As flight commander, Lockhart continued to do his share of the work, successfully navigating his Lysander to an old airfield in the Auvergne, east of the town of Ussel and close to the limit of the aircraft's range. Here he collected Leon Faye of the Alliance network. A few days later, on 31 August 1942, he set off again, this time for a field among the vineyards of Burgundy. This mission would end with the Lysander's undercarriage shattered by a ditch which ran two-thirds of the way along the flare path chosen by his French reception committee. He, like Nesbitt-Dufort, was fortunate to escape capture after being stranded in France, and eventually escaped from a beach near Narbonne to a Royal Navy-operated felucca, which carried him and other French Resistance members to Gibraltar.

By this time No 161 Squadron had six Lysanders at its disposal, plus one in reserve, to meet the increasing demand for pickups in France. The web of intelligence agents and Resistance cells was continually growing along with the need to ferry key individuals in and out of Britain for high-level briefings, for training or simply to provide sanctuary from the Gestapo. Whereas in the early days there may have been one or two operations during every moon period, by the end of 1942 this had increased to as many as 20 if the weather was favourable. A string of individuals of appropriate skill and character were now drafted in to fly these missions.

They ranged widely in age and experience. The tall, laconic, jazz-loving 19-year-old Peter Vaughan-Fowler had applied and been selected after the signal asking for volunteers had omitted the word 'night' in its intended specification of 'at least 250 hours of night-flying experience'. He had less than 250 hours in total under his belt but proved to be a very fast learner, completing 26 missions without mishap before his eventual redeployment as a Mosquito pilot.

On the other hand, John Bridger – older than the other pilots and a man of few words – was a highly seasoned recruit with 4,000 hours of flying already behind him. He, too, ended his time with the squadron unscathed after a dozen sorties, although only his handling skill saved him on one occasion in April 1943. His Lysander overran the plateau designated for his landing south of Clermont-Ferrand and, in his desperate attempt to become airborne again, he hit the crest of the ridge beyond, destroying one of the tyres of his undercarriage and flying through high-tension cables between two pylons. Recovering his vision from the blinding flash this had caused, he brought his plane round again and made a successful landing. In order to take off from the field on an even keel, he punctured his one good tyre with several shots from his pistol. His eventual landing back at Tangmere was uneventful in spite of the punctured tyres, except that 7m of thick copper wire could be seen trailing behind him as he touched down on the tarmac.

Frank 'Bunny' Rymills, a veteran of 26 bombing raids and 24 clandestine parachute drops, was still only 21 when he joined the Lysander flight. On the ground, he was inseparable from his cocker spaniel, Henry. A former student of architecture and an avid beekeeper, Rymills was also a skilled poacher, the mentality for which must have suited the nocturnal stealth and daring required of a Lysander pickup pilot. He only spent six months with the squadron, but still carried out 12 operations, ferrying some 30 agents in or out of France.

On one occasion, in June 1943, Rymills forgot to switch off his radio transmitter while communicating with his two female passengers,

Cecily Lefort and Noor Inayat Khan, as they flew over the French coast on their way to a landing site near Angers. Possibly to calm their nerves, he was pointing out how beautiful it looked in the summer moonlight and identifying towns and other landmarks to them. This was a double Lysander operation and it was with considerable horror that James McCairns, his fellow pilot, endured more than 30 minutes of this running commentary over his headphones, knowing that the Germans would be listening to every word. Fortunately Rymills's indiscretion did not affect the safe completion of the mission, and all four outward-bound agents (McCairns was carrying Charles Skepper and Diana Rowden) were successfully spirited away to take up the various assignments they had been given by the Special Operations Executive. Tragically, however, not one of this quartet would make it back to Britain. All were eventually caught and tortured by the Gestapo; Cecily Lefort never returned from Ravensbrük concentration camp, Noor Inayat Khan was executed at Dachau, Diana Rowden at Natzweiler, and Charles Skepper also died in Germany from the injuries inflicted by his captors.

James McCairns, or 'Mac' as he was known, had joined the Lysander flight in the autumn of 1942. Still only 23, he had flown a Spitfire as a sergeant-pilot in Douglas Bader's renowned

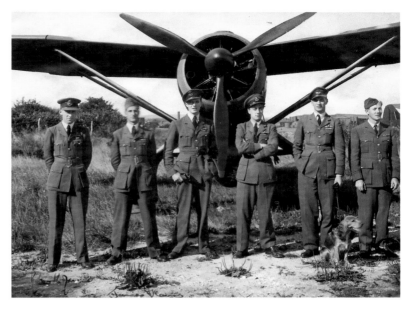

No 616 Squadron. McCairns's service alongside the legendary pilot that he so greatly admired was cut short in July 1941 when he was shot down, wounded and captured by the Germans. By the following January he had recovered sufficiently to make a successful escape from his prisoner-of-war camp in Germany and had reached Belgium. Thanks to the Belgian underground and MI9's escape organisation in Europe, McCairns was smuggled to Gibraltar and returned to the UK. During his concealment

ABOVE Pilots of
**No 161 Squadron in
the summer of 1943,
from left to right:
Robin Hooper, Jimmy
McCairns, Peter
Vaughan-Fowler, Hugh
Verity, Frank ('Bunny')
Rymills and Stephen
Hankey.** *(Bertram family)*

LEFT Flying Officer
Jim McCairns standing
between his rigger
and his fitter and in
front of his Lysander
Mk IIIA (V9622 'MA-E')
at Tempsford.** *(Andy
Thomas collection)*

in Belgium he had heard about the black Lysander operations and at one point was expecting this to be his way out of occupied Europe. Back in service with the RAF, he became determined to repay those who had helped him escape by volunteering as a pickup pilot.

As a non-commissioned pilot with limited flying hours due to his incarceration, his application was scrutinised closely by the Tempsford commander, 'Mouse' Fielden. However, the understanding he had gained of how the Resistance worked while he was on the run stood him in good stead and he was taken on. The decision was undoubtedly vindicated, as McCairns went on to complete 25 successful pickups and earned the DFC and MM, even though his second operation on 22 November 1942 led to his being temporarily suspended. It was a double Lysander mission with Peter Vaughan-Fowler and, as with all double missions, there was a strict rule that either both planes should land at the target or neither. Furthermore, Vaughan-Fowler, as the senior pilot, should land and take off first.

It was quite a short trip to the east of the Seine, between Rouen and Paris, but there was low cloud and patchy fog over France and the landing site was difficult to locate. The two pilots lost sight of each other as they searched for the agent's signal and radio contact was fitful. McCairns mistakenly thought that

Vaughan-Fowler's brief and indistinct message that he was setting course for home meant that he had landed successfully and exchanged his passengers. Therefore, when he spotted the correct signal, he brought his plane down and was disconcerted to hear from the reception party that the other Lysander had never put down. Five people were waiting on the ground for their flight to England, and the decision was taken to cram four of them into the Lysander cockpit – the first time such a number had been carried. Amid all the recriminations McCairns encountered on his return to Tangmere for having unintentionally disobeyed orders, he was able to take some comfort in the fact that the four he had rescued were Max Petit, an important operator in the *Confrérie de Notre Dame* network whose cover had just been blown, his wife and their two young sons. In fact, although he did not know it at the time, the Gestapo arrived to arrest the family only one day after their airlift to safety.

The man responsible for disciplining McCairns was the newly appointed commander of No 161 Squadron, Wing Commander Percy Pickard. 'Pick', as he was universally known, was 27 and already a highly distinguished figure in the RAF, and seemed a good ten years older to his contemporaries. He had earned the DFC, the DSO and a bar flying bombers and had led the famous parachute raid on the German radar station at Bruneval on the French coast near Le Havre in February 1942. He went on to become the first RAF officer to win a second bar to the DSO in 1943 as a result of his work as a Lysander and Hudson special duties pilot. Pickard's face was also well known outside the RAF, because he had appeared as the pilot of 'F' for Freddie, a Wellington bomber featured in an Oscar-winning 1941 documentary, *Target for Tonight*. He was a tall, heavily built man with very fair hair and a pointed nose. He was seldom seen out of his cockpit without his pipe and his Old English sheepdog, Ming.

He clearly also believed in taking some home comforts with him on operations. In January 1943 he was returning from a field near Issoudun with the former French ambassador to Turkey, René Massigli, and André Manuel, Passy's right-hand man in the Free French intelligence service. To his great concern,

BELOW Wing Commander Percy ('Pick') Pickard (in the centre with his dog Ming), commander of No 161 (Special Duties) Squadron, who was later killed during the celebrated air raid on Amiens Prison in February 1944. *(IWM)*

he could not recognise where he was as he crossed the French coastline. Trusting his compass, he carried on across the Channel, but as his fuel gauge continued to fall, there was no sign of land ahead. At last, with the needle on empty, a rugged coastline appeared: it was the southernmost tip of Cornwall. Fortunately there was an RAF airfield at Predannack, near Lizard Point, and he made it down without a drop of fuel left in the reserve tank. It transpired that the Lysander's compass had been affected by a metallic object in one of Pickard's flying boots. It might have been the bayonet he carried there, or it could have been the stainless steel whisky flask he had shoved into the top of his boot after a fortifying swig.

As well as doing his fair share of Lysander pickups, Pickard was the man to demonstrate the suitability of the larger Hudson for moonlit landings in France. He developed the technique of bringing the aircraft in to land at a speed much slower than the 75 knots recommended in the pilot's handbook, and needing only 350yd to pull up on landing. He then flew No 161 Squadron's first successful Hudson mission in February 1943, bringing seven agents back from a field south-east of Arles in the Midi. It was only a year later when, as the leader of a Mosquito squadron, he was part of the daring Operation Jericho, a bombing raid on Amiens prison to free Resistance fighters condemned to death by the Gestapo. Although the raid succeeded, Pickard was caught from behind by a German fighter plane as he left the scene, his tail was severed and he and his navigator died as the plane turned turtle and crashed to the ground. He left a wife, Dorothy, and a one-year-old son.

Pickard's new Mosquito command and the posting of Peter Vaughan-Fowler to fly in the same squadron, together with other impending departures, meant that replacements were required for Lysander special duties in the later months of 1943. They came in the shape of four men: Jim McBride, Robin Hooper, Jimmy Bathgate and Stephen Hankey. Jim McBride, a tall, muscular but shy man, was a product of Strathallan School in Scotland and St Catherine's College, Cambridge, who left university to join the RAF in 1940. His flying experience had been with Wellington bombers

over much of Europe. Robin Hooper, an Oxford graduate who had learnt to fly with the university air squadron, had entered the Foreign Office before the war but had persuaded his masters to let him pursue active service with the RAF when hostilities began. He had already been carrying out special duties with No 138 Squadron, parachuting agents and supplies as a Halifax pilot.

Jimmy Bathgate was a small, fair-haired New Zealander, an accomplished pilot and a scrupulously careful navigator. In ten missions between September and December 1943, he carried 27 passengers in and out of France. On the night of 10 December he set out from Tangmere on a double Lysander operation with Capitaine Claudius Four on board, an important coordinator of the Resistance in central France. Jim McBride was flying the other aircraft and their target was a field near Laon, to the north of Reims. The weather was very poor and it was no surprise to the ground crew at Tangmere when McBride reported a failed mission on his return. To their mounting concern and ultimate dismay, the second Lysander did not return home that night. No one knew what had happened and it was only six months later that news came out of France that Bathgate's plane had been shot down near a German night-fighter base at Juvincourt on the Laon to Reims road. Both he and his outward-bound passenger had been killed.

It was after sombre events such as Bathgate's failure to get home that pilots of the squadron looked to the most flamboyant of their number, Stephen Hankey, to lift them from their gloom. If his patrician demeanour gave the brief impression of a Bertie Wooster, it was soon dispelled by his sharp and outrageous wit and a resourcefulness which would not allow the strictures of his and his fellow pilots' military life get in the way of their well-being. 'Any bloody fool can be uncomfortable,' he would say as he arranged, against all regulations, to install his wife and two young daughters in a cottage close to Tangmere. He had made a similar arrangement at the beginning of the war, finding a flat in Paris for his wife so that he could make frequent visits from his posting with one of the army cooperation Lysander squadrons which took such a battering over northern France prior to Dunkirk.

Hankey felt very much at home at Tangmere, having been brought up as the youngest son of a distinguished Sussex family in a large country house, Binderton, on the other side of Chichester from the aerodrome. Barbara Bertram, a long-standing friend of the family and nine years Stephen's senior, had watched him growing up and was delighted to welcome him, along with the other Lysander pilots, to her impromptu parties at Bignor Manor. The Hankey family had, in fact, vacated Binderton House during the war and loaned it to their friends Anthony Eden and his wife Beatrice, who used it as a retreat from the exigencies of a wartime Foreign Office. On one occasion, Hankey invited the Edens over to tea at The Cottage in Tangmere. After he had given him a guided tour of their establishment and introduced the pilots, Eden confessed that he had no idea that 'all this' was going on. As he was Foreign Secretary, everyone roared with laughter.

Hankey's flying career had only begun after a short spell in the army, which had marked him with a broken nose sustained while boxing at Sandhurst, and which sometimes gave him agonising sinus pain when at the controls of a plane. After trying his hand as a salesman of Delahaye sports cars in London he joined the RAF, and, following his traumatic tour of duty in France, was sent to the Middle East to train Allied aircrew cadets. Each button on his RAF tunic was from a different air force as a memento of this work. At 28 he came to No 161 Squadron, older than most newcomers and with very little night-flying experience. He trained hard, however, to come up to the standard of his fellow pilots and flew his first mission, a successful pickup to the west of Paris, on 14 September 1943. Tragically, however, he and Jim McBride would not see another Christmas.

The December moon of 1943 had not begun well for No 161 Squadron. The first operation was the one from which Jimmy Bathgate never returned, and then bad weather forced two further missions to turn back unfulfilled. One of these had been an attempt by the squadron's commander, Wing Commander Bob Hodges, to pick up one of his own men, Robin Hooper, who had been stranded in France since the previous moon, when his plane had become irretrievably bogged down in a field near Niort in western France.

On the night of 16 December the weather was better and the forecast promised a clear passage to and from France, although there was a slight chance of some fog forming on the English south coast later in the night. Hodges therefore made preparations once again for a flight to a field some 40 miles south of the Loire, near Parthenay. His outward passenger was an agent for the Belgian government in exile, François de Kinder. Meanwhile, a second operation, entitled Diable, was also planned for the same night using two Lysanders, in which Stephen Hankey and Jim McBride would return Georges Charaudeau, the head of the SIS's Madrid-based network, Alibi, to the French countryside near Chateauroux, along with five of his fellow agents.

All three pilots were in a hurry to get off that night so as to beat any fog on the return journey. In fact they set off so early that when Bob Hodges began to circle over the French landing site the reception party were only just arriving, and he had to wait while they hastily set up the flare path. The landing, exchange of passengers, take-off and homeward flight passed without incident and in the clearest of moonlit visibility. But approaching the English coast, instead of the dark shape of land, a thick, white blanket lay spread out beneath them. Tangmere radioed to them that there was currently about 500ft of moderate visibility beneath the cloud but that it was deteriorating rapidly. Relying on his instruments alone, Hodges made his blind approach to the runway as the Lysander descended through some 1,000ft of dense fog. The ground appeared suddenly 300ft below them, allowing the pilot just enough time to adjust his approach for a conventional runway landing.

Delighted though he was to have successfully retrieved one of his squadron's top pilots from potential torture and death at the hands of the Gestapo, and to have got home in the nick of time, Hodges could not celebrate. The other two Lysanders were still on their way home and the cloud base was falling all the time. He made for the control tower where both Hankey and McBride were already in radio contact as they approached across the Channel. With thick ground fog imminent all along the south coast of England, planes returning from operations all over the Continent were being diverted to Woodbridge in Suffolk, where visibility was slightly better and where special paraffin burners were in place along the runway to disperse the fog.

But that was no option for the two Lysanders, whose fuel tanks were close to empty. In other circumstances Hodges would have been happy to order his two pilots to sacrifice their aircraft and to bail out. But their passengers – they had two each – were without parachutes, so they had somehow to bring their planes down intact. As they were both due overhead at roughly the same time, Stephen Hankey was told to land at the neighbouring naval airfield at Ford while McBride began his approach on Tangmere. With both pilot and control tower relying entirely on instruments, McBride was guided on to his final approach. Visibility on the ground was now only 500yd, but he arrived over the end of the runway at the perfect altitude and heading for landing. At this moment, however, he saw the red light on the top of the runway controller's caravan and mistook it for hangar obstruction lights. He radioed sharply, 'You are flying me into the hangars', and opened up the throttles to go round again. Once more, he came in on a final approach, receiving assurances from the controller that he was set for a successful landing. Then the radio went dead. No plane emerged from the fog; there was utter silence.

Hodges, Hooper and several others made their way to the end of the runway and then began to cross the heavily ploughed fields that lay under the final approach path. Eventually they saw an orange glow through the fog which, as they drew close, became the sight they had been dreading – a fiercely burning Lysander on its nose, the pilot trapped in the cockpit and obviously dead. A man and a woman stood beside the wreckage, clearly in shock and utterly disoriented. These had been McBride's passengers, Marcel Sandeyron, a garage owner from Pont de Vaux on the Saône who worked for the *Azur* network, and a female agent known only by her code name, Atalas. They had miraculously survived the crash unscathed and were later taken back to Bignor by Tony Bertram.

This was only after Tony had carried out an even more unenviable task. He had been called to a hillside to the west of Ford aerodrome where Stephen Hankey's aeroplane had hit a tree as he attempted to land. Tony had been asked to identify the three charred bodies in the wreckage, as he was likely to have known them all. Apart from his close friend, the pilot, there was Albert Kohan (alias Berthaud), a White Russian turned Free French Resistance leader who, on his earlier wartime visits to England, had become hugely popular with both the pilots and the SIS conducting staff. The third corpse was of another previous visitor to London, Jacques Tayar (alias Cazenave), leader of the *Electre* intelligence network and a pivotal player in the radio communications systems set up between France and London.

The man whose memoirs we have to thank for so much of this information about the Lysander moonlight flight is Hugh Verity who, having qualified as one of its pilots in November 1942, simultaneously became its commanding officer at the tender age of 24. The son of an Anglican clergyman, educated at Cheltenham and Queen's College, Oxford, where he read French and Spanish and learnt to fly with the university air squadron, he joined the RAF when war was declared in 1939. By the time he volunteered for the special duties squadron he had flown bombers with Coastal Command and spent a year as a night-fighter pilot. These postings had not been enough to convince him he had yet quelled the demons of physical cowardice that had beset him on the rugby fields of Cheltenham, and he was determined to prove his courage in the lonely night skies over enemy territory.

Although his book, *We Landed by Moonlight*, never makes it obvious, it is easy to deduce that this calm, courteous and competent airman commanded great respect from the unconventional group of pilots for whom he was responsible. He flew more missions than any of them during his time in charge and made as many life-long admirers among the French Resistance men and women as he did among his RAF peers. His book makes it very clear how important the bond was between the Lysander and Hudson pilots and the agents responsible for their reception on French soil. The chances were that the pilot and agent in charge of a landing would know each other well because they had trained together in England. Warm greetings took place up at the pilot's cockpit in the brief minutes of a passenger exchange and generous black market gifts of wine and perfume were thrust into the pilot's hand.

Hugh Verity had established a particularly strong relationship with one of the SOE's most trusted and frequently called-upon agents, Henri Déricourt. Déricourt, himself a skilled aviator, had

RIGHT Flying Officer Norman Attenborrow of No 148 Squadron based at Brindisi on the south-east Italian coast. In September 1944 he flew his special duties Lysander Mk IIIA 500 miles across the Adriatic to German-occupied Greece on a mercy mission. A wounded American officer, John Giannaris, with only about 12 hours to live without specialist medical attention, had been waiting for several days at a partisan airstrip not far from Karditsa to be picked up, but low cloud had prevented it. Attenborrow succeeded, however, in penetrating the cloud to land and (right) the invalid was laid out in the Lysander's rear cockpit and flown without incident back to Brindisi. The American survived the flight and recovered from his wounds in hospital. (Andy Thomas collection/IWM C3132)

come to Britain in 1942 via Spain and Gibraltar thanks to the MI9 escape network and hoped to secure a job flying for BOAC. The MI5 vetting process for newly arrived foreigners channelled him towards the SOE, however, who took him on in spite of a somewhat equivocal report on his credentials. The Frenchman clearly had great charm and easily convinced Maurice Buckmaster, head of the SOE's F Section, to give him responsibility for organising their agents' arrivals and departures in France. Déricourt's beguiling nature was such that Hugh Verity was moved to write to his wife at the end of their pickup training together to say: 'I have a very good friend called Henri. I have given him your telephone number and told him that you would do whatever you could to help him, no matter when. Don't forget, Darling, even if he rings up after several years, to think of him as an old friend of mine. You will find him very nice.'

It is now widely believed that Déricourt was a traitor. His trial in Paris in 1948 failed to convict him, and this was partly because his SOE masters seemed so reluctant either to believe in or admit to his duplicity. None of them gave evidence against him and one, Nicholas Bodington, appeared in his defence. German records have nevertheless shown him to be in the pay of the *Sicherheitsdienst*, the SS security service, and one of its officers had borne witness to his dealings with them. An even darker theory that Déricourt was a triple agent, secretly working for the SIS who were happy to sacrifice agents of the SOE to the Gestapo, as they had been fed false information about where and when the Allied invasion was planned, has yet to be convincingly proved.

The sense of betrayal must have been doubly bitter for Hugh Verity; not only because of his fondness for the man but also because he discovered that, on each of the 18 occasions that Déricourt had led the reception committee for Lysander pickups, he and the other pilots had been delivering brave men and women to their near-certain capture, torture and death. The lucrative deal that Déricourt struck with the Germans meant that, while the planes were allowed to land and take off unscathed, he would supply details of every incoming and outgoing flight and individual on board. (The quartet flown out by Rymills and

McCairns in June 1943 were probably victims of his treachery.) He also made copies of all the messages due to be flown back to London and passed them on to the Germans.

The safe passage granted the unwitting Lysander pilots on some of their flights made them no less courageous. They understood very well the kind of fate that might await them if they were caught on enemy soil, especially as the war lengthened and stories got back about the Gestapo's methods of extracting information. It was only by sheer good fortune and by the bravery of those who sheltered them that every pickup pilot stranded in France evaded capture and eventually made it home. By the end of the Lysander special duties into France in 1944, five more pilots besides Jimmy Bathgate would lose their lives, however – victims either of bad weather or enemy fire. Compared with other RAF wartime operations, the ratio of such losses

to successful missions was remarkably favourable and a testament to the skill and daring of the men who flew them.

After the invasion of Normandy in June 1944 the work of No 161 Squadron changed as aircraft larger than the Lysander, such as the Hudson, could be used to ferry more people into France via airfields already liberated by the advancing Allies. The last successful special duties Lysander mission by the squadron was carried out on the night of 5/6 August when Squadron Leader Len Ratcliff brought back an American airman who had been shot down near Bourges in central France.

Another squadron, No 148, was assigned special duties at the beginning of 1944 in southern Italy, with four Lysanders operating from a base in Brindisi. At first the pilots, among them Peter Vaughan-Fowler, were sent on assignments to Yugoslavia, in cooperation with the partisans, and to Greece

LEFT A sequence of events behind enemy lines in northern Italy in April 1945. Top left: a special duties Lysander is surrounded by partisan fighters just after it lands in a field near the town of Cortemilia. *(IWM NA 25412)* **Top right: the pilot (right) and the British liaison officer attached to the partisan group (left) discuss what is required.** *(IWM NA 25413)* **Bottom left and right: three of the partisans, wounded in an engagement with local fascists, one of them seriously, are loaded into the rear cockpit before being flown to safety.** *(IWM NA 25414, 25415)*

Noor Inayat Khan

Shortly after her birth to a princely Indian Muslim father and an American mother in Moscow in 1914, Noor Inayat Khan moved with her family to London just before the outbreak of the First World War. When she was six the family moved again, to France, but in June 1940 her now widowed mother escaped with her children back to England as the Germans invaded. By now Noor was an accomplished children's author, but in spite of her father's strong pacifist beliefs she became determined to involve herself in the war against the Nazis.

Having joined the Women's Auxiliary Air Force where she trained as a radio operator, that skill, coupled with her fluent French, made her a natural candidate for the F (French) Section of the Special Operations Executive. She began her training in February 1943 and was flown, with three fellow SOE passengers – Diana Rowden, Cecily Lefort and Charles Skepper – to a moonlit field in northern France in a double Lysander operation the following June. She travelled to Paris to join the *Physician* network as a radio operator, and almost immediately found herself to be its sole link

ABOVE AND BELOW
Post-war service: Lysander V9867, (complete with long-range fuel tank) of No 357 Squadron having put down at Bolo Auk landing strip in Burma in late 1945 in order to collect a Marschal Schen and his wife (below) and fly them back to the squadron's base. This aircraft later met with a mishap when its undercarriage gave way on landing at one of the uneven jungle airstrips in the region.
(RAF Museum)

where a watch was needed over the warring resistance factions. In June the Lysanders were moved to Corsica, where they undertook missions behind enemy lines in northern Italy and France where, in August, they became extremely busy in the run-up to the Allied landings in the south of France.

A flight of special duties Lysanders were also used by No 357 Squadron in Burma in 1945 in cooperation with SOE activities behind the Japanese lines. These missions were fraught with difficulty for the pilots, who too frequently found that the rudimentary jungle landing strips got the better of the Lysander's undercarriage. Eight aircraft were wrecked during these operations, four of which mishaps occurred after Japan's unconditional surrender on 14 August while the pilots were engaged in leaflet dropping and assisting the process of the laying down of arms.

BELOW Noor Inayat Khan, a heroine of SOE.
(IWM HU 74868)

with London after the arrest of all other operators and many other members of the network.

For four months Noor survived a cat-and-mouse existence in Paris as she evaded the German radio detector vans and the Gestapo security officers who had been supplied with an accurate description of her. Whether her eventual betrayal and arrest on 13 October 1943 was down to the notorious double agent Henri Déricourt or the jealous sister of another French agent is uncertain. The result, however, was interrogation at the Gestapo HQ at 84 Avenue Foch (from which she made two unsuccessful escape attempts), imprisonment in Germany, where she was kept in chains, and ultimate execution by a shot in the back of the head at Dachau concentration camp on 13 September 1944. In all the time of her incarceration she gave away nothing about her fellow agents.

Noor Inayat Khan was posthumously awarded a British George Cross in 1949 and a French Croix de Guerre avec étoile de vermeil.

Wing Commander F.F.E. Yeo-Thomas, GC

Forest Frederick Edward Yeo-Thomas was born in 1902 in London to English parents who moved with their son to Dieppe in France when he was still young. Yeo-Thomas therefore grew up bilingual and, after a period in the army fighting alongside the Poles in the 1919–20 Polish–Soviet war, when he escaped capture and imminent execution by the Soviets, he took up a business career in Paris.

But the invasion of France in 1940 prompted him to flee to London, where he soon found useful employment acting as an interpreter at General de Gaulle's Free French headquarters. Before long, however, he was recruited by the SOE to serve as a liaison officer with the French intelligence service, the *Bureau Central de Renseignements et d'Action* (BCRA), set up by de Gaulle in London. Yeo-Thomas forged strong links with the head of the BCRA, André Dewavrin (code name alias Colonel Passy), and one of de Gaulle's key Resistance organisers in France, Pierre Brossolette. In so doing he bridged the usually turbulent divide between the SOE and the British Secret Intelligence Service, who would normally claim first call on Passy and his organisation, especially in the earlier years of the war.

Along with Brossolette, Yeo-Thomas became a frequent flier with the special duties squadron, based at RAF Tempsford, returned to France for the first time via a parachute drop in February 1943, and exfiltrated again in a Lysander operation three months later with Passy and Brossolette as fellow passengers. In September of the same year he was sent back to France for two more months

with the task of equipping and aiding the cohesion of Resistance forces. Both outward and return passages were by Lysander. He was delivered by parachute for his final mission into France in February 1944, but he had been betrayed and was soon in the hands of the Gestapo in their Paris headquarters.

Not only did he survive the most brutal beatings and torture, including near drowning in ice-cold water and electric shocks to his genitals, he made two failed attempts to escape from Fresnes prison in Paris, where he was held until he ended up in Buchenwald concentration camp. There he helped to organise resistance within the camp and, through collusion with one of the German doctors, saved himself and two other prisoners from execution by swapping identities with three inmates who had died from tuberculosis. He escaped from a work party outside the camp and when recaptured passed himself off as a French prisoner of war and was sent to a POW camp near Marienburg. From this camp he led two daring escape attempts. The first, in April 1945, was in broad daylight, and ten of the twenty escapees were shot by prison guards as they fled. Yeo-Thomas was recaptured after nearly a fortnight on the run and only 800 yards from American lines. A few days later he led a party of ten men out of the camp, through enemy lines and to safety.

Wing Commander Yeo-Thomas was awarded the George Cross, the Military Cross and Bar, the Légion d'Honneur (Commander) and the Croix de Guerre at the end of the war.

BELOW Wing Commander F.F.E. Yeo-Thomas, GC.
(Copyright unknown)

Chapter Five

The Shuttleworth Lysander

A star of the famous Shuttleworth Collection of airworthy veteran aircraft, Lysander V9367, bearing the black livery of 161 (Special Duties) Squadron, draws admirers from far and wide to the regular air displays at Old Warden. Restored from an abandoned ex-Royal Canadian Air Force Lysander, the Shuttleworth 'Lizzie' is kept in peak flying order by a dedicated team of engineers.

OPPOSITE The Shuttleworth Lysander (V9367, G-AZWT) displays at Old Warden airfield in September 2008. *(PRM Aviation Collection)*

There is an ultimately rather sad postscript to the extraordinary clandestine work of No 161 Squadron and the courageous individuals who were ferried in and out of France during her dark days of occupation. Phillip Schneidau, the first SIS agent to be brought out of France by a special duties Lysander in October 1940 (see previous chapter), was working at the British embassy in Paris immediately after the war. He, together with the British ambassador, Duff Cooper, arranged for a ceremony to take place at Les Invalides that is described by Tony Bertram in the introduction to his wife Barbara's account of her part in the operations, *French Resistance in Sussex*:

'On the twenty-seventh of January 1946, in the Cour d'Honneur of the Invalides, the British Ambassador presented a Westland Lysander to the French Air Ministry. By this symbolic act the secrecy was lifted from a remarkable series of operations and a most personal and dramatic relationship between a group of British officers and the French Resistance was enshrined.

'This Lysander belonged to a Flight which, from October 1940 until the Liberation, had regularly landed in occupied France to establish the two-way traffic that was necessary to supplement the one-way traffic of the parachute.

'We stood facing it in two groups. One was of those pilots, operators and passengers who had survived, many of them still haggard from torture and prison; the other of British officers who had

organised these complex operations or trained the French operators. Among them was my wife, whose part in the affair had been unique.

'Between these groups and the aircraft there paraded, of course, the high-ranking officers and officials who are always so prominent on such occasions and so innocent of their significance. Flanking it were detachments of the Royal Air Force, the Armée de l'Air and the Garde Républicaine, with bands and standards. In this way the gawky old aircraft, that had often rested on French soil for two or three minutes in an obscure field, was consigned for ever to a French museum, a pensioner among pensioners.

'After the last flourish of trumpets and the march past and when the generals had gone, the two groups mixed and went off to the celebrations which were to last for some of us until three o'clock the next morning. The aircraft was left in the drizzle, under the sagging cloud that recalled so many anxious days when the telephone announced "Operation Off" ... "C'est off".'

In 1961 Barbara Bertram and her son, Jeremy, visited Les Invalides and enquired of the whereabouts of the Lysander presented to the French nation 15 years earlier. They were, in Jeremy Bertram's words, 'rather fobbed off'. It was left to a descendant of another SIS conducting officer and regular visitor to Bignor Manor, John Gentry, to uncover the fate of the aircraft. Gentry's daughter, Caroline, and more particularly her husband, Jean-Jacques Babois,

RIGHT Lysander Mk IIIA, '2363', is flown by the Canadian Warplane Heritage Museum in Ontario. *(PRM Aviation Collection)*

with the advantage of living in France, carried out some determined research. In his book, *Secret of Bignor Manor*, Jeremy Bertram relates what Babois discovered:

'For a start, that particular Lysander had never flown in an operation. It was number V9614, built as a Mk IIIa target tower used for maintenance until it was issued to No 161 Squadron on 13 August 1944, found to be damaged on delivery and returned to No 5 Maintenance Unit three days later.

'After its solemn presentation, it was exhibited for some time in the Champs-Elysées along with other Allied military material. It was then taken into store at Bernes, by being towed along the roads (without its wings) despite the severe over-heating this caused the wheels, never designed for such work. No longer airworthy, it was stowed away until, in June 1949, it went for scrap along with other old aircraft. No one had remembered that it was supposed to go to the Musée de l'Air.'

It does appear that innocence of its significance by high-ranking officers and officials, (to use Tony Bertram's phrase), might well have led to V9614's eventual unfortunate disposal. General de Gaulle, famous for his lack of willingness to acknowledge the role of the British Secret Service in aiding the Resistance, can probably not be blamed for this particular erasure of a historical artefact, as he had resigned his premiership a week before the presentation. Not that he would probably have advocated its preservation had he been consulted.

Even if no surviving Lysander is on show on French soil, there are still several that can be seen on public display around the world. It is not surprising, perhaps, that Canada is the source of most Lysanders we can see today. Most of the 225 Mk IIs and IIIs built there under licence never saw actual combat and many were disposed of soon after the war, often sold at a knock-down price to farmers who used them for crop-spraying.

At the last count there are two Lysanders in flying condition and on display in Canada itself: one, finished in the broad yellow and black striped livery of a target tug, at the Canadian Warplane Heritage Museum in Ontario, and the other, silver-painted similar to the prototypes flown by Westland's back in 1936, at Vintage Wings

LEFT Sabena Lysander Mk IIIA (2442, 'OO-SOT'), seen at Duxford in July 1994. *(PRM Aviation Collection)*

CENTRE The RAF Museum's Lysander (R9125) on static display at Hendon. *(PRM Aviation Collection)*

of Canada, at the Gatineau-Ottawa Executive Airport, Quebec. Two other museums display static versions, namely the Canada Aviation and Space Museum in Ottawa, and the Canadian Museum of Flight in Langley, British Columbia.

In the United States the Udvar-Hazy Center near Dulles International Airport, the Smithsonian Institution's adjunct to the National Air and Space Museum, displays a Lysander Mk IIIA in night-flying camouflage to replicate an RAF special duties aircraft from No 138 Squadron. Another Lysander can be viewed at the Florida Air Museum on the south-west corner of Lakeland Linder Regional Airport.

On another continent, the Indian Air Force Museum at Palam, New Delhi, houses a Canadian-built Lysander Mk III, while back in Europe there is an ex-RCAF version maintained to airworthiness by volunteers of Sabena Airlines' Old Timers and current personnel.

In the United Kingdom there are three restored Lysanders on view to the public. One, a Mk III in the army cooperation colour scheme of No 225 Squadron, is at the RAF Museum in Hendon, North London. The Imperial War Museum at Duxford in Cambridgeshire displays another Mk III, this one marked as being of RAF Tempsford's special duties No 161 Squadron.

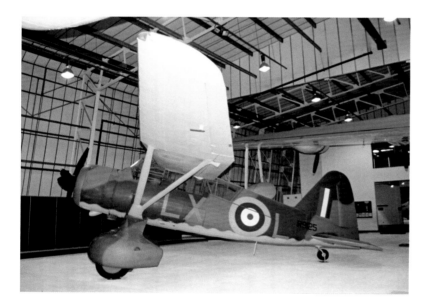

The Shuttleworth Collection

It is at the Shuttleworth Collection at Old Warden airfield in Bedfordshire that the only airworthy Lysander in the UK can be seen,

LEFT The Imperial War Museum's Lysander Mk IIIA is presented as V9673, 'MA-J', a special duties 'Lizzie' flown by Squadron Leader Hugh Verity, CO of No 161 Squadron's Lysander Flight at RAF Tempsford in 1943. *(PRM Aviation Collection)*

taking regularly to the air on their special air days, and viewable at close quarters at all other times in the display hangar.

The collection of more than 50 airworthy and predominantly original veteran aircraft is named after the last of the line of the Shuttleworth family, which lived at Old Warden Park from the 1870s for nearly 100 years. Richard Shuttleworth, born in 1909, inherited the family fortune and country estate when he was 23. He demonstrated a passion for all things mechanical from a very early age, and this led to him participating in motor racing and, in 1935, winning the first British Grand Prix at Donington Park. He took part in races all over the world until the 1936 South African Grand Prix, where he crashed and injured himself badly enough to decide to quit motor racing. Instead he turned to his other great love, aviation, which was deemed a safer occupation.

Tragically, Shuttleworth died at the controls of an aircraft in 1940 after he had joined up with the RAF. His Fairey Battle crashed into a hillside during a night-flying training exercise. By this time he had built up and restored a sizeable collection of vintage cars and aircraft at Old Warden, and his mother, Dorothy, was determined that his memory would live on in the preservation of the collection. She therefore set up the Shuttleworth Trust, which has continued, since her death in 1968, to sustain the collection and to support education in aviation and agriculture (another of Richard's keen interests).

The Shuttleworth Lysander, officially

registered G-AZWT by the Civil Aviation Authority, was acquired in 1998 from a dispersed collection of vintage aircraft that had been put together by Sir William Roberts of Strathallan, near Auchterarder in Perthshire. The Strathallan Collection, as it was known, had been set up in the early 1970s and acquired aircraft – mainly of Second World War vintage – from all over the world. Unfortunately the collection, which, like Shuttleworth, aimed to keep as many of its exhibits as possible in an airworthy condition, was forced to close as a public attraction in 1980 through lack of funds.

Sir William Roberts had bought a version of the Lysander for his collection in 1971 from Wes Agnew, a Canadian farmer and former wartime pilot. Agnew, realising there would eventually be a market for historic aircraft, had garnered a

ABOVE A general view of the grass airfield at Old Warden in Bedfordshire, home to the Shuttleworth Collection of historic aircraft. *(John Harding)*

LEFT Abandoned to the elements on a Canadian farm: a veteran of the RCAF and how the Shuttleworth Lysander might have looked before its salvage by Wes Agnew in 1971. *(Copyright unknown)*

ABOVE V9281
'RU-M', V9673 'MA-J'
(Imperial War Museum,
Duxford), and V9367
'MA-B' (Shuttleworth
Trust), at the Imperial
War Museum, Duxford
in July 1995. (PRM
Aviation Collection)

number of ex-military planes, originally sold out of service at the end of the war by the RCAF and acquired by farmers for crop dusting and other agricultural purposes. It took some eight years for the Strathallan Collection to bring the restoration of the Lysander IIIA in their care to the point of airworthiness, but it eventually flew again in 1979, painted to represent V9441, AR-A, of the RAF's No 309 (Polish) Squadron.

Records show that the aircraft was flown (albeit somewhat infrequently due to problems with the Mercury engine) until 1987, when it was kept dry-stored at Strathallan for the next ten years. It was then flown down to Duxford aerodrome, where the Aircraft Restoration Company was able to sort out the engine

problems prior to its sale to Shuttleworth. For the first two years of its time at Old Warden the Lysander flew in the colours it had been given at Strathallan, but in 2000 the livery was changed to the all-black night camouflage of RAF Tempsford's No 161 Squadron. A dummy long-range fuel tank was fixed to the underbelly and the additional oil tank behind the pilot's head, together with the side ladder to the rear cockpit, were installed to fully replicate a special duties Lysander. To complete the effect, it was given the identity of V9367, MA-B. This was the plane flown by Peter Vaughan-Fowler on Operation Apollo in November 1942, when he brought three Corsican police inspectors out of southern France after they had helped Marie-Madeleine Fourcade, head of the *Alliance* intelligence network, escape from a Vichy prison.

Of course, the true origins of the Shuttleworth Lysander are not quite so romantic and are a little bit uncertain. The aircraft sold by Wes Agnew to Sir William Roberts was, as far as can be ascertained, a Mk III built in Yeovil by Westland in 1942 (constructor's serial no Y1536) and shipped to Canada in June of that

LEFT A rare sight and one that will probably never be seen again – a Lysander three-ship: V9545, 'BA-C' (Wessex Aviation and Transport), V9441, 'AR-A' (2442, 'OO-SOT', Sabena), and V9367, 'MA-B' (Shuttleworth Trust), flying at Duxford in June 1998. (PRM Aviation Collection)

RIGHT **V9367 in the workshop at Old Warden in**
May 1999 before she was repainted in the overall
black special duties colour scheme which she
wears today. *(PRM Aviation Collection)*

CENTRE **Black-painted V9367 seen at Duxford in**
July 2003. *(PRM Aviation Collection)*

year as part of the British Commonwealth Air
Training plan. The Royal Canadian Air Force
gave the plane a different serial number, 1582,
and converted it to a target tug in December
1942. It was sold out of service in 1946.

The uncertainty lies in the fact that when the
Strathallan Collection first registered the plane
its previous identity was shown as 2355, which
is the RCAF serial for a different, Canadian-built,
Mk III target tug, one of the 150 constructed at
the National Steel Car Corp at Malton, Ontario.
This plane was sold directly out of service to
Wes Agnew in 1946. However, at the time the
restored Lysander was re-registered in 1998,
prior to its sale to Shuttleworth, its earlier
identity was shown to be 1582, the Westland-
built version. The probable explanation for this
apparent dual identity is that Wes Agnew had
used a few parts bearing the 2355 identity from
another Lysander in his collection to make up a
complete aircraft to sell to Sir William Roberts.
Therefore during its rebuild at Strathallan it was
thought to be the Canadian-built model because
the 2355 number was found on some of the
parts. It was only later, through corresponding
with Agnew, that they ascertained the bulk of
the machine was indeed the Yeovil-built Mk III.

Whatever the explanation, thanks to the
dedicated group of engineers at Old Warden
airfield this Shuttleworth Lysander, G-AZWT,
makes an admirable airworthy example of her
type, and allows every visitor to the collection
to picture precisely how this short take-off
and landing aircraft played such an important
part in the secret war behind enemy lines in
Continental Europe.

RIGHT **V9367 in close formation with the**
Shuttleworth Trust's other high-wing army
cooperation aircraft, the Second World War vintage
German Fieseler Storch. *(PRM Aviation Collection)*

Chapter Six

The pilot's view

────●────

Although regarded with affection by her wartime pilots, the Lysander is not a simple aircraft to fly. Even the official RAF pilots' handbook criticises the controls as not being 'well harmonised' and the unusual need to adjust the tail-plane before take-off and landing is crucial to its safe operation. A 21st century test-pilot goes through the take-off routine and explains what the Lysander is really like to fly.

OPPOSITE Shuttleworth pilot Keith Dennison runs through his cockpit checks in the collection's Lysander. *(All photos John Harding unless credited otherwise)*

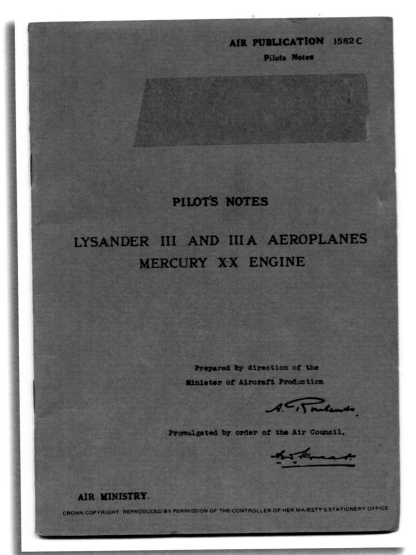

AIR PUBLICATION 1582 C
Pilots Notes

PILOT'S NOTES

LYSANDER III AND III A AEROPLANES
MERCURY XX ENGINE

Prepared by direction of the
Minister of Aircraft Production

Promulgated by order of the Air Council.

AIR MINISTRY.

CROWN COPYRIGHT. REPRODUCED BY PERMISSION OF THE CONTROLLER OF HER MAJESTY'S STATIONERY OFFICE

Picture a young man, possibly not yet out of his teens, in unbuttoned blue RAF tunic, reclining on his bunk, and, open in his hand, a thin grey-coloured booklet which he is reading with profound concentration. The title of the booklet is: *Pilot's Notes – Lysander III and IIIA Aeroplanes, Mercury XX Engine.* The notes are dated July 1941, and additional words on the front cover state that they have been prepared 'by direction of the Minister of Aircraft Production' and 'promulgated by order of the Air Council', with the facsimile signatures of their respective permanent secretaries beneath. Our pilot will have just arrived for his training on the Lysander, and an assimilation of the booklet's content is what could mean the difference between life and death for him.

It is the same booklet that Hugh Verity of special duties fame used when he sat in the Lysander cockpit to teach himself, not only to fly the plane but to know all the drills by heart, and all the controls by touch alone, in preparation for night flying. It is, as he recalls in *We Landed by Moonlight*, 'a very simple pilot's manual compared with others I have studied since'.

Its first five pages take the reader through the controls and equipment in the cockpit, each of which is enumerated and pointed out in photographs at the back. The rest of the pages are given over to notes about flying and handling the aircraft. The writing style is terse and some passages about the Lysander's

ABOVE Pilot's notes for the Lysander Mk III and Mk IIIA. *(Shuttleworth Collection)*

RIGHT A Lysander Mk II (N1256) of No 225 Squadron practising formation flying over the English countryside in the months before the Battle of France in 1940. *(PRM Aviation Collection)*

idiosyncrasies must have made a young pilot sit up and pay particular attention through its critical tone. For instance, the note entitled 'General flying' states: 'The controls are not well harmonised, the rudder being light, ailerons heavy and elevator too heavy at or near maximum angle.'

Before any instructions, however, comes a list of minimum and maximum operational limitations. These include maximum rpm and cylinder temperature allowable for take-off, climbing, cruising and in emergencies. The minimum rpm for take-off is 2,180, the maximum, when diving, is 3,120, but only for a 20-second burst. Speed in a dive must not exceed 300mph.

With the limitations out of the way, the business of getting the aircraft under way is addressed. The instructions read as follows:

PRELIMINARIES
On entering the cockpit, close the hood and side panels and see that the brakes are on.

STARTING THE ENGINE AND WARMING UP
Set:

a. Throttle – ½ inch open.

b. Mixture control – NORMAL.

c. Airscrew pitch control – pulled out for coarse pitch.[1]

d. Fuel cock – ON.

e. Gills – fully OPEN.

f. Carburettor air intake heat control – pushed in for cold.

g. Priming cock – PRIME CARBURETTOR.

■ Unscrew and operate the priming pump until a sudden increase in pressure is felt.

■ Turn the priming cock to PRIME ENGINE.

■ Give the engine 4 strokes of the priming pump if hot or 8 if cold. At the same time with the ignition switches OFF, turn the engine by electric starter or by hand until priming is completed.

■ Close the priming cock and screw down the priming pump.

■ Switch ON the main ignition switches and the starting magneto.

■ Press the starter button. (The starter should not be used continuously for more than

10 seconds with an interval of at least 10 seconds between each attempt.)

■ As soon as the engine is firing evenly, switch OFF the starting magneto and turn on the oil heating by pulling out the control knob.

■ Let the engine tick over slowly for about 5 minutes, then open up to a fast tick over until the oil inlet temperature has reached 5 degrees C.

■ During warming up, the carburettor air intake heat control may be pulled out to admit warm air during cold weather, but it must be pushed in to admit cold air before opening up the engine.

■ Before opening up, push in the oil heating control knob.

TESTING ENGINE AND INSTALLATIONS

■ While warming up, make the usual tests of temperatures, pressures and operation of controls. Brake pressure should be at least 100 lb/sq.in. After a few minutes, the airscrew control should be pushed in to fine pitch.[2]

■ After warming up, open up to about 1800 r.p.m. and then change to coarse pitch. This should cause a large drop in r.p.m. Then return to fine pitch and the r.p.m. should return to 1800.

■ Open up the throttle to the CRUISING position and check each magneto for even running. The drop in r.p.m. should not exceed 100.

■ Open the throttle fully and check boost, oil pressure and r.p.m.; the latter should be 2500–2600.

[1] Author's footnote: This particular instruction is a handwritten alteration on the original typescript, which tells the pilot to do the opposite, *ie* to push the control in for fine pitch. Similar instructions on starting the engine in the Lysander technical handbook also prescribe the fine pitch setting, and in Hugh Verity's account of his own run-up routine he also starts the engine with the propeller in fine pitch. Shuttleworth pilot, Keith Dennison, explains why the instruction was changed and is still adhered to today: 'We always start in coarse pitch, and to achieve this we always select coarse pitch while taxiing in after landing. The landing itself is, of course, flown in fine pitch. Fine pitch is selected after a few minutes of idling after start, and the run-up is conducted in fine pitch with a check of the propeller's operation to coarse and back to fine as part of the run-up checks. The reason for the procedure of closing down and starting in coarse pitch is that with the propeller in coarse there is no oil in the propeller hub. Thus the oil is warmed in the engine during the early running of the engine and then warm oil is injected into the hub to effect the move to fine pitch after a few minutes. If you close down in fine pitch then the propeller hub is left full of (isolated) oil which does not get warmed by the early running of the engine. This can result in a situation where the cold (and therefore thick) oil in the propeller refuses to move when coarse pitch is selected, and this can result in an aborted sortie. In the worst case, if the pilot isn't diligent about his pre-take-off checks, the problem can go unnoticed until after take-off, and then the sortie has to be aborted due to the inability to get the propeller into coarse.
[2] Additional handwritten sentence.

Pilot's instrument panel key

1 Triple pressure gauge
2 Airspeed indicator
3 Artificial horizon
4 Rate of climb and descent indicator
5 Landing lights switch
6 Pitot head switch
7 Magneto switches
8 Altimeter
9 Directional gyro
10 Turn and slip indicator
11 Fuel pressure gauge
12 Boost gauge
13 Cylinder temperature gauge
14 Engine speed indicator
15 Oil pressure gauge
16 Oil temperature gauge
17 Bomb selector switches (inoperative)
18 Flap over bomb jettison push button
19 Bomb jettison master switch
20 Flap over container jettison push button
21 Airscrew pitch control knob
22 Carburettor slow-running cut-out control knob
23 Rudder bar control knob
24 Air temperature gauge (behind control yoke)
25 Generator
26 Fuel priming pump
27 Cockpit floodlight dimmer switch
28 Oil heating control knob
29 Cockpit heating control knob
30 Carburettor air intake heat control knob
31 Three-way priming cock
32 Starting magneto switch
33 Engine starting push button (underneath flap)
34 Control column
35 Gun selector control button
36 Brake control and parking lever

ABOVE Shuttleworth pilot Roger ('Dodge') Bailey talks through the engine start procedure for the Lysander.

First I check the rudder bar is adjusted to me.

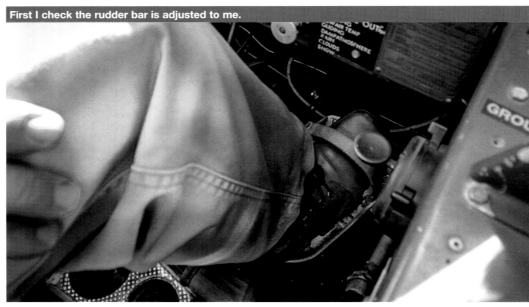

Then the elevator and the aileron.

Wheel brakes I can check ...

... and the trimmer.

Round the cockpit – throttle shut, mixture normal.

Fuel cock open.

Ignition off.

Propeller pitch cock pulled out – coarse pitch at this stage.

I'm now going to unscrew the primer.

Select 'prime carburettor' ...

... and rotate the primary cock.

Clear the guard for the starter.

I'm ready to start the engine.

I now prime. I do that until I get the fuel pressure.

Then I rotate the priming cock to 'prime engine'...

... and I'm going to prime again.

And then it would be a matter of getting the throttle shut, booster on, ignition on.

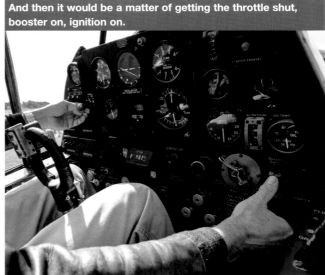

Booster control goes down and start her up.

And then the engine is running and I'm looking for 100° on the cylinder head temperature or thereabouts ...

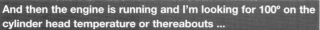

... and looking for the oil pressure to stabilise at 80. That tells me that the high initial oil pressure valve is closed and the engine is warm.

Now I'm ready to do the engine run-up and the first thing I will do is push fine pitch ...

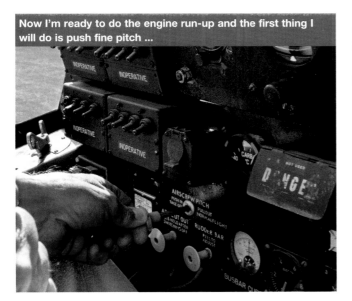

... and then set the throttle to zero boost.

Then exercise the propeller by pulling the cock out ...

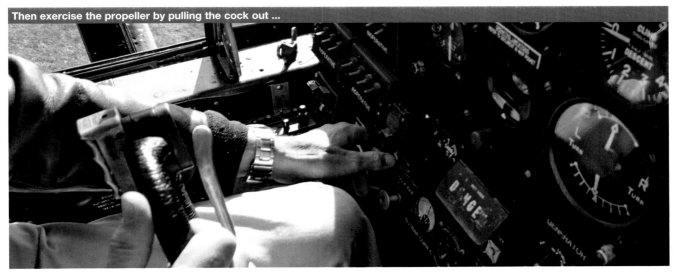

... and checking the rpm change.

Now I check each magneto in turn.

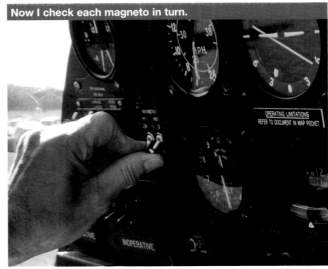

Then throttle back and check that it's idle – I'm looking just for a smooth idle.

The last thing I need to do is reset this trim to the take-off position.

We've done the engine run-up now so it's the pre-take-off check – the usual one – trim, pitch of prop to 'fine', mixture control to 'normal', fuel on ...

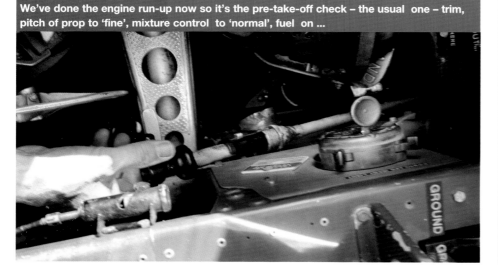

... gills open ...

FINAL PREPARATION FOR TAKE-OFF – DRILL OF VITAL ACTIONS

Drill is 'T.M.P. fuel and gills'.

T – Tail actuating wheel
    set pointer to TAKE-OFF.

M – Mixture control – NORMAL.

P – Pitch – Control pushed in for fine pitch.

Fuel – ON.

Check contents of tank. The fuel gauge is just aft of the pilot to port and can be seen by him if the aperture in the armour-plated bulkhead is open. There are two calibrations on the gauge, one for tail down and one for flying position. The gauge is not reliable below 15 gallons.

Gills – OPEN.

TAKING OFF

- The take-off is normal and there is little tendency to swing. The tail should not be lifted.
- Do not start to climb until safety speed of 80 m.p.h. A.S.I.R. is reached.

- A steep angle of climb can be obtained by climbing at 70 m.p.h. or even down to a minimum of 60 m.p.h. This is an emergency operation and should only be performed if necessitated by operational considerations. If engine failure occurs while climbing at this speed, the nose must be pushed down instantly, otherwise at least 600ft will be lost before control is regained.

ENGINE FAILURE DURING TAKE-OFF

- Fully wind back the tail actuating gear wheel.
- Push the nose down and glide at 80 m.p.h. as close to the ground as possible.
- Switch OFF the ignition and turn OFF the fuel.

CLIMBING

- The best climbing speed with the throttle in the CRUISING position is 110 m.p.h. and the aeroplane must not be climbed continuously at less than this speed.

ABOVE **Climb.** *(PRM
Aviation Collection)*

Having dealt with the practicalities of getting the Lysander airborne, the *Pilot's Notes* take on an even more schoolmasterly tone. Under the 'General Flying' heading, it is easy to read into the text the anguish suffered by those responsible for teaching young men to fly the Lysander in its early days, when the false security engendered by the aircraft's slow flying capabilities led to a number of fatal crashes:

The flying characteristics at very low speeds are such that a foolhardy pilot might be tempted to take liberties to which no aeroplane can with safety be subjected. Particular reference in this respect is made to stalled take-offs and climbs, stalled approaches to land, and low flying at too low an airspeed. The stall is delayed to an exceptionally large angle of attack, and can seldom be reached. But if this aeroplane does stall, a wing drops very sharply and control is entirely lost until speed is regained after loss of 1,000 feet.

A single sentence under the heading 'Spinning and Aerobatics' is categorical:

Spinning and aerobatics are not permitted.

Some notes follow about diving, including the need for coarse pitch on the propeller, to avoid sudden manoeuvres at high speed and to wind back the tailplane wheel slightly when travelling at more than 250mph. Then comes the most important part of all – getting the plane back down on the ground.

APPROACH AND LANDING
■ Reduce speed to 120 m.p.h. and check brake pressure. As soon as the engine is throttled back, the aeroplane becomes very nose heavy.
■ The gliding speed can be varied to as high as can be desired down to about 70 m.p.h. At about this speed the aeroplane has a very high rate of descent and only gentle turns should be attempted, care being taken not to stall. At about 80 m.p.h. the glide is much

flatter and turns up to about 45° may be made with safety.

- On a straight glide, when the speed drops to about 85 m.p.h., the inner slats will open a little, this lowering the flaps to a certain extent. The lower the speed is below this point, the more the flaps will be lowered, and therefore the steeper the glide. At about 95 m.p.h. the inner slats will be closed and the flaps will be fully retracted, thus allowing the gliding angle to be comparatively flat.
- The aeroplane can be sideslipped up to any normal degree of bank.
- Carry out the drill of vital actions 'T.M.P'.
  T – Tail actuating gear – wind back until aeroplane will fly 'hands off' at 75–80 m.p.h.
  M – Mixture control – NORMAL.
  P – Pitch – Control pushed in for fine pitch. The automatic operation of the flaps causes them to take up their own position for the various conditions of flight.
  At normal approach speed, 80 m.p.h., they will be approximately half down.
- Engine assisted approach and landing – Approach at 80 m.p.h. with engine running at about 1200 r.p.m. This will provide ample float while holding off. The landing is straightforward and the flaps come down

fully as the aeroplane flattens out and slows down to a landing speed. The throttle should not be finally closed until flattening out has been completed. Care must be taken not to hold off too high. The brakes may be applied, gently at first, soon after landing.
- Glide approach – Correct speed 85 m.p.h.

Three additional paragraphs conclude the pilot's notes. The first deals with a mislanding – the situation that worried original test pilot Harald Penrose the most about the inherent safety of the Lysander. The notes instruct the pilot to maintain flying speed while the tail actuating wheel is wound forward. On no account, they state, should the throttle be opened fully with the wheel wound back.

Although landing a Lysander in a crosswind can be made satisfactorily, the notes continue, it should not be attempted if the surface wind exceeds 20mph.

Finally, the reader is told that after a landing the cowling gills should be opened fully and then, while taxiing in, the propeller should be changed to coarse pitch. Once at a standstill the pilot should pull out the jet cut-out control to stop the engine, turn off the main ignition switches and turn off the fuel cock.

LEFT Taxiing. *(PRM Aviation Collection)*

RIGHT Richard Hillary, Battle of Britain Spitfire pilot and erstwhile Lysander pilot. *(Copyright unknown)*

BELOW Hillary had trained as an army-cooperation pilot on Lysanders at Old Sarum before the shortage of trained pilots in the Battle of Britain saw him posted to a front-line Spitfire squadron. This is a Lysander Mk I (L4742, 'TV-B') of No 4 Squadron on army cooperation training in mid-1939. *(Andy Thomas collection)*

How would our young pilot have felt as he climbed down from the cockpit having completed his first flight in control of a Lysander? One such Second World War pilot was 21-year-old Flying Officer Richard Hillary, whose very first posting after learning to fly with the RAF was to Old Sarum, home of the School of Army Cooperation. It was the spring of 1940

and Hillary had been bitterly disappointed not to have been chosen as a fighter pilot, having instead been selected to fly what one of his fellow young pilots termed a 'flying coffin' – although that was before he had even set foot in a Lysander.

As it turned out, at the end of his six-weeks' training at Old Sarum Hillary and most of the others on his course were told that they were needed as Spitfire pilots. The threat of a German invasion after the fall of France had become so great that more fighters were urgently required. Hillary would go on to distinguish himself in the Battle of Britain until September 1940, when he was shot down over the Channel, miraculously surviving terrible burns to his hands and face and three hours in the water before the Margate lifeboat picked him up.

A flying accident while he was at the controls of a night-fighter two years later ended his young life, but not before he had completed a highly acclaimed account of the uncertain life of a Battle of Britain pilot, *The Last Enemy*. It is this book that allows us a brief insight into the training of an army cooperation pilot. 'The work at Old Sarum was interesting,' he recalled. 'We studied detailed-map reading, aerial photography, air-to-ground Morse, artillery shoots and long-distance reconnaissance. The Lysander proved to be a

ponderous old gentleman's plane, heavy on the controls but easy to handle. It seemed almost impossible to stall it.'

Clearly Hillary was not a man to heed every paragraph of the pilot's notes, particularly the one that states 'spinning and aerobatics are not permitted'. 'Of flying incidents there were few,' he recounted, 'though once I did my best to kill my observer. We were on our way back from a photography sortie when I decided to do some aerobatics. As our Inter-Comm was not working, I turned round, pointed at the observer, and then tapped my straps, to ask him if he was adequately tied in. He nodded. I started off by doing a couple of stall turns. Behind me I could hear him shouting away in what I took to be an involuntary excess of enthusiastic approval. After the second stall turn I put the machine into a loop. On the dive down he leaned forward and shouted in my ear. I waved my hand. On the climb up, I saw him out of the corner of my eye letting himself low down into the rear seat. Then we were up and over. I straightened up and looked back. There was no sign of my observer. I shouted. Still he did not appear. I had a sudden feeling of apprehension. That shouting – could it mean ...? I peered anxiously over the side. At that moment a white face emerged slowly from the back cockpit, a

hand grabbed my shoulder and a voice shouted in my ear: "For Christ's sake don't do a slow roll, I'm not strapped in!"

'He had taken my signals for a query whether I was strapped in. His cries had been not of joy but of fear, and when we had started down on our loop he had dived rapidly to the bottom of the cockpit, clutching feverishly at the camera on the floor for support and convinced that his last hour had come.

'I headed back for the aerodrome and, after making a quick circuit, deposited him gingerly on the field, landing as though I had dynamite in the back.'

If Hillary got away with a cavalier disregard for the rulebook, another Lysander pilot, later in the war, encountered catastrophe in a moonlit French field probably because he overlooked one of its 'vital actions' in preparation for a landing.

It was the night of 10 February 1944 and a young Australian, Flying Officer John McDonald, was on his way to a clandestine landing site to the south-east of Bourges in central France. It was only his third mission and he had three French intelligence agents squeezed into the rear cockpit. On reaching the appointed field, McDonald aborted his first and second approaches and hit the ground at great speed on the third, running on beyond the flare path

BELOW Although this photograph was taken in peacetime some 40 years after the events described in 1944 involving Flying Officer John McDonald, it serves to illustrate that the 'Lizzie' could sometimes be a handful to land safely. Luckily, in this case the pilot survived the forced-landing of V9281 on 21 August 1983 at Witchford, when the aircraft overturned. (PRM Aviation Collection)

into a ploughed field, where the Lysander flipped upside down and burst into flames. Two of the agents were thrown out of the rear cockpit more or less unscathed while the pilot and the other passenger were trapped in the burning fuselage. The reception party were beaten back by the heat of the fire and were forced to leave the scene before the Germans arrived to investigate the blaze. In fact the third passenger did manage to clamber out of the wreckage, badly burned, and made it to a local village, where he was cared for and hidden. Flying Officer John McDonald did not survive.

Having heard the circumstances of the accident from the pilot of the other Lysander on this double aircraft mission, McDonald's colleagues back at RAF Tangmere sadly concluded that he had possibly forgotten one of the 'vital actions' prior to landing as listed in the *Pilot's Notes*: if he had not put the mixture control from 'WEAK' to 'NORMAL' he would have been unable to throttle back completely and would have landed too fast.

By the safety standards of 21st-century flying, how much unnecessary or unjustifiable risk did the RAF put in the way of its young Lysander pilots of the Second World War? It is, of course,

unfair to condemn 1930s technology in the light of what we know today, but it is interesting to be able to ask two highly experienced pilots of the jet age about the aircraft's characteristics, both good and bad.

The Shuttleworth Aircraft Collection at Old Warden Park has a unique asset in that it attracts pilots of the highest calibre to fly its historic planes (all of which are airworthy – a prerequisite for any aircraft being accepted into the collection). The chief Shuttleworth pilot, Roger ('Dodge') Bailey, has been flying since 1969 and has been involved with the museum since 1988, when he was serving in the RAF as a test pilot at the Royal Aircraft Establishment at Bedford. He has an intimate knowledge of all the aircraft in the collection, not least the Lysander, which has played a starring part in the air days there since its acquisition in 1998.

Asked how straightforward he finds the Lysander to fly compared with a modern propeller plane of similar proportions, he replies:

'There are very few modern propeller aircraft of similar proportions. In terms of handling it is a bit like a Pilatus PC-6, but obviously the power plant arrangements are very different and less "carefree".'

The aircraft has plenty of power for the role, he finds, and 'it cruises quite fast, and is surprisingly manoeuvrable, although control forces are high when compared to a fighter of the same era. The view is excellent.'

The Lysander's brakes are what he finds most troublesome about the aircraft, as they seem to lack effectiveness and can fade following prolonged use in crosswind operations. Comparing the relative difficulties of flying the Lysander with other military aircraft of a similar vintage, 'Dodge' Bailey says that it is different rather than more difficult:

'The flaps and slats are "automatic", and there is no cockpit control lever for them. The pilot must understand that the high-lift devices operate only by angle of attack – which in turn is controlled only by the elevator angle. Fore/aft stick movements will cause the angle of attack to decrease/increase, which in turn causes the high-lift devices to retract/extend. This arrangement provides a sort of "direct lift control" or "flight path control" which is somewhat unconventional. If the pilot attempts to fly the approach using the now fashionable "point and power" technique he will struggle to fly a stable approach path.'

Harald Penrose, the original test pilot for the Lysander, was unhappy about allowing the aircraft into production with the adjustable tailplane, fearing its wrong deployment would cause accidents. Would 'Dodge' Bailey have shared his concerns?

'Many aircraft have trimmable tailplanes, especially when required to cope with a wide range of centres of gravity. Contemporary aircraft such as the Gladiator and Hind had trimmable tailplanes, so Harald Penrose was not against trimmable tailplanes per se, but rather the amount of adjustment that was required on the Lysander to counter the nose-down pitching moments of the high-lift devices inter alia.

'His concern was an overshoot (a go-around, in modern parlance) from a landing when the tailplane had been trimmed up fully and then high power added. The tailplane is set low and gets the full benefit of the energised prop-wash increasing the downforce generated by the tailplane setting, thereby forcing the nose up. Then, when the pilot attempted to stop the nose rising with the elevator, he would find that there was insufficient elevator control power to overcome the nose-up pitch and control would be lost. Since full power is never required to go-around the simple answer is to apply the power in manageable stages and re-trim the tailplane between each stage. Interestingly modern passenger jets suffer from the same problem and it still causes accidents every now and then – usually by an unthinking pilot using too much power and not understanding fully that the tailplane will generally beat the elevator if the tailplane is not re-trimmed during the go-around.'

For a pilot preparing to take a Lysander up for the first time, as well as earlier comments, Bailey has the following advice:

'Do your weight and balance calculations carefully. Understand how the engine and propeller works. Get a competent engineer to brief you on engine starting. Make sure the tailplane is set for take-off before you leave the chocks. Do not attempt to raise the tail wheel on take-off – allow the aircraft to fly off in the three-point attitude.'

And on the Lysander's reputation of being virtually impossible to stall, he observes:

'The aircraft does not reach a conventional stall as such so we use a minimum in-flight speed of 60mph. An attempt to force a stall with power has been shown to result in a complete loss of control and a very significant loss of height. If you have a need to fly very slowly, or to maximise climb rate, set the two-pitch prop to fine pitch; in all other circumstances coarse pitch can be set at 100mph after take-off and left there until base leg.'

Keith Dennison is another distinguished pilot whom Shuttleworth is fortunate to count among its number. Flying solo as a glider pilot at the youngest permissible age, his 16th birthday, he had gained his private pilot's licence just after his 17th birthday with the help of an RAF flying scholarship and a full year before he had learnt to drive a car. His subsequent career in the RAF included six years as a Phantom FGR2 pilot, and after three tours of test flying at Boscombe Down he became Chief Test Pilot at the establishment. He flew and tested all of the RAF's fast jet aircraft and trainers and many large aircraft, including the Hercules. He also test flew helicopters. After leaving the RAF he became the Chief Test Pilot for BAE Systems, responsible for all fast jet and trainer testing, and flew the Hawk and the Typhoon. He started vintage display flying in 1990 with what is now known as the Great War Display Team, and has been flying for the Shuttleworth Collection since 2000.

BELOW Keith Dennison, Shuttleworth pilot.

THE ART OF ENTERING THE LYSANDER COCKPIT

THIS PAGE Keith Dennison does the mandatory walk-round of the aircraft to check all is well.

THIS PAGE He places his right foot in the foothold in the wheel fairing and reaches for the lift strut to pull himself up and on to the wheel fairing.

137

THIS PAGE Then he places his left foot forward onto the step. and using the lift strut again as a foothold, and the foothold in the fuselage side below the cockpit sill, he pulls himself up ...

LEFT ... and is now able to climb down and into the cockpit.

LEFT After running through cockpit checks and start-up procedure (see pages 120–26) the Lysander is ready to taxi.

Keith Dennison is in no doubt that the Lysander is more difficult to fly than any comparable modern plane. This, he explains, 'is due to its quirky handling qualities, which would not pass a modern certification; some serious handling traps that will kill you; and an engine that, while powerful, requires careful handling'.

If that sounds severe, Dennison clearly has a soft spot for the aircraft:

'The Lysander was one of the first kits that I bought as an aeroplane-mad youngster. I was, and remain, fascinated by the shape of the aircraft and its resemblance to a dragonfly. There really is nothing else that looks like it. Apart from that I enjoy flying the aircraft as it is quirky and a challenge, and to put on a good, safe display in the aircraft requires you to be on top of your game.'

So what makes it quirky and a challenge, even for an aviator of his experience and skill?

'The most surprising and troublesome aspect of the aircraft is that the view from the cockpit, although very good for viewing the ground, is quite poor when you are looking around you, and particularly up and behind. The aircraft was designed as an army cooperation aircraft, so the emphasis was placed on a good view downwards, but the concomitant positioning of the wing at the pilot's eye-line does not help when looking for other aircraft. This is particularly an issue in formation displays. The other issue that gives cause for caution is that the brakes are very weak and are prone to fading very easily, this, in turn, gives marginal directional control on the ground.'

Keith Dennison is firmly of the opinion that the Lysander is more difficult to fly than other military aircraft of a similar era and requires a greater degree of care: 'If you treat it as just another aeroplane, as you can with other contemporary aircraft, then it will kill you.'

And he does not mince his words when asked about Harald Penrose's doubts about allowing the aircraft into production with the adjustable tailplane:

'Mr Penrose was very right to be concerned. The tailplane trimming system can be lethal and was the cause of numerous accidents and fatalities in service, but the exigencies of war took priority. I have said before that the Lysander flown without care will kill you. Specifically, it is the tailplane trimming system that will kill

you. The problem is that the trimming system causes the angle of the whole tailplane to change. This makes the trimming control very powerful, particularly when full power is applied and the tailplane is fully enveloped in the high-speed jet of air aft of the propeller. Against this characteristic is the fact that the elevator on the Lysander is very small and relatively far less powerful in generating pitching moments than the tailplane trimming system.

'The upshot of these design characteristics is that the Lysander pilot needs to be extremely careful to ensure that he has the tailplane trim correctly set for each phase of flight. The two specific danger times are take-off, where, if the trim is left at its normal ground setting of fully aft as opposed to the proper take-off trim position, the aircraft will pitch up uncontrollably after lift-off leading to a stall and crash tail-first. The other dangerous manoeuvre is an overshoot from an approach. On the approach to land the tailplane is trimmed full aft on finals to ensure sufficient nose-up pitch authority for the flare and landing (the middle part of the finals turn is consequently usually flown out-of-trim with a substantial push force). If, for any reason, the approach needs to be aborted and an overshoot flown then the correct technique is to apply a little power, then three handfuls of the big trim wheel, a little more power, three more handfuls of trim and so on until the aircraft is climbing away in trim. There are about 12 handfuls of trim from the approach setting to the take-off/overshoot settings, so the overshoot is a long, disciplined and slightly tense process that cannot be rushed. If the pilot panics and simply applies full power without moving the trim then, again, the aircraft will rear up uncontrollably, even with the pilot pushing the stick fully forward, until the aircraft simply runs out of forward speed and falls to earth.'

The issue of tailplane trimming is the first thing Keith Dennison would point out to a first-time Lysander pilot. But he would also make them aware of significant pitfalls in handling the engine:

'The engine is very prone to carburettor icing, so it is very important to monitor the carburettor air intake temperature and adjust the air intake control to maintain the temperature, if possible, above 10°C; this is rarely possible, so looking at the temperature is always a worry.

'Negative g, or even just an abrupt nose-

down pitch, can cause the carburettor to make the mixture too rich and the engine will hesitate or, in the worst case, stop. Pilots must avoid abrupt nose-down pitch inputs.

'The accelerator pump on the carburettor is very powerful and can easily cause the mixture to become too rich and rich-cut or stop the engine. It is vitally important that all engine accelerations are smooth and progressive.

'Both of the last two points are particularly pertinent when trying to fly formation for display purposes. Operationally, the carburettor icing issue was clearly a worry for winter operations, and the issue of rapid throttle movement compounded the difficulties of performing an overshoot, perhaps from above a field in darkest France.

'Lastly, the pilot must think through the characteristics of the aircraft on the approach as, with no cockpit controls for the flaps and slats, which are completely aerodynamically controlled, the aircraft has approach characteristics unlike any other. Usually, if the approach is a little high, the solution is to take some power off and lower the nose until the approach angle is correct and then reapply the power and raise the nose to establish the new approach angle. In the Lysander, if the approach is high and if the normal technique is applied then as the nose is lowered (which lowers the wings' angle of attack) the slats move in, the flaps move up and the drag of the aircraft reduces, so the aircraft accelerates. The pilot does not want to pull off too much power because he knows that he must reapply the power very slowly or risk a rich-cut, so the aircraft descends but accelerates.

'When the pilot achieves his desired approach angle he now (gently) reapplies the power and raises the nose (increasing the wing angle of attack); in response to the increasing angle of attack the slats move out and the flaps move down, but with the aircraft flying faster than it was. The result of the extra speed and the high-lift devices deploying is that there is an excess of lift and the aircraft floats upwards. The upshot of this application of normal technique to being slightly high on the approach is that the aircraft usually ends up at an even higher approach angle than it was to start with. The correct Lysander technique in this situation is to reduce power but, counter-intuitively, raise the nose, which causes the slats and flaps to move further out and down, and this in turn increases the drag on the aircraft. The drag causes an increased rate of descent which can be held until the desired approach angle is achieved, then a small reapplication of power and a slight lowering of the nose will re-establish a stable approach at the new, correct, approach angle. You really have to think through the Lysander before you go and fly it; trying to figure all this out while you are flying is too late.'

Dennison's final observation is that: 'The aircraft has quite low directional stability and a very light rudder and these combine to make it quite hard to keep the aircraft in balance at all times. But compared with everything else that the pilot must keep at the fore-front of his mind, this is a small thing which can be mastered with some experience and practice.'

Chapter Seven

The engineer's view

What does it take to keep a 70-year-old warplane airworthy? Shuttleworth's chief engineer explains the challenges of finding or re-manufacturing spare parts and maintaining the aircraft to the required standard for its 'Permit to Fly'. His annual list of checks, inspections and servicing is shown here in detail.

OPPOSITE Last-minute snag rectification is carried out on the Lysander's Bristol Mercury engine before a flying display at Old Warden. *(All photos by John Harding except where credited otherwise)*

On 24 March 1943, Sergeant Sam Hollis of No 161 Squadron's Lysander Flight ground crew received this note from his Squadron Leader, Hugh Verity:

'Dear Sam,
So far this has been our most successful month. I want to congratulate the Flight on the fine show you have all put up, and thank you all for your enthusiasm and initiative. The aeroplanes have been very operational and smart as well. Not one flight has been spoilt by bad maintenance nor one take-off delayed. While most of the congratulations go to the pilots, we all feel that they should be passed on to the boys. Thank you and keep it up!
Sincerely,
Hugh Verity, S/L'

The fact that the successful pilot is only as good as his ground crew is as true today as it was in the days when men and machines were put under so much pressure behind enemy lines. At least for the likes of Sergeant Sam Hollis there existed an entire infrastructure to enable effective maintenance and to supply spare parts for the Lysander Flight of No 161 Squadron. Today, to keep a Second World War aircraft airworthy there are very specific challenges for the team of engineers responsible for maintaining the Shuttleworth Lysander.

Jean-Michel Munn is Chief Engineer at Shuttleworth, and as such is in charge of the maintenance of every aircraft in the collection. He began his time at Old Warden as a volunteer mechanic while earning a living working with light aircraft. Then, after about two years, a vacancy became available and Munn spent the next ten years helping to maintain all the Shuttleworth aircraft on the workshop floor. He became Chief Engineer in 2007. Here he answers some questions about keeping their Lysander in working order.

Firstly, how much help are the maintenance notes, produced in 1939, in carrying out the necessary procedures to satisfy today's CAA standards?

'Our maintenance schedules are based on the original manufacturer's schedules, which are amended to take into account the significantly different operational conditions we have today. The original schedule is based purely on flying hours with few calendar requirements, as it was designed for a front-line aircraft in daily use which would fly hundreds of hours a year in all weather conditions.

'In contrast our usage is less than 20 hours a year, generally in dry conditions, and the aircraft is kept hangared at all times when not in use. Therefore we are more concerned with age-related than wear-related deterioration. The original servicing and inspection requirements are adjusted to suitable calendar times, with additional requirements that take into account the age of the aircraft, modern maintenance practices, regulatory requirements and, of course, our own experience. The maintenance and inspection schedule is necessarily subject to regular review and amendment.'

What is the most troublesome aspect of maintaining the Shuttleworth Lysander?

'Excluding accidental damage, there are very few issues with the airframe. We have experienced internal corrosion in some of the structural elements of the fuselage. The automatic slat/flap mechanism needs careful setting up but little ongoing attention. The brakes cause perhaps the biggest issues on the airframe. They are a poor design that gives a poor braking effect, and they readily overheat. They are designed as an aid to taxiing rather than to reduce the landing roll, but even so they are liable to fade rather quickly on a windy day when they are needed to keep the

BELOW A Shuttleworth engineer up to his wrists inside the Mercury engine.

aircraft from weather-cocking into wind (the Lysander has large rear fuselage and fin areas and a relatively small rudder). The rubber brake actuating bags are quite a complex/tricky item to re-manufacture, and we currently have no spares of these.

'The Bristol Mercury engine is a superb piece of machinery, built to a very high standard and generally very reliable and durable. The main problems we have are largely age- or corrosion-related. Bristols made extensive use of magnesium castings, which are very lightweight but can suffer very badly from corrosion. The upper cylinder assemblies suffer from age-related issues that shorten the valve gear life. The main issue with the aero piston engines, especially the higher power later types, is that they are very complex and make use of highly developed processes and materials. They were, as are the modern jet engines today, at the cutting edge of technology and therefore very expensive items to produce and consequently even more expensive to reproduce.

'The propeller is reliable and pretty much trouble-free, but corrosion and spares are an issue. Even the smallest damage and corrosion in the critical areas of this highly stressed item would render it irreparably unairworthy. Currently we have no spares of the major components (blades, hub and spider).

'Probably the biggest ongoing problem that affects the serviceability of the aircraft is the complex exhaust system, which consists of an annular ring mounted to the engine and connected by articulated stub pipes to the 18 exhaust ports. The ring itself forms the front of the engine cowl. There are two types: a nickel-plated mild steel type which readily corrodes in the extreme environment of the hot and corrosive exhaust gases, and a corrosion-resistant stainless (Inconel) type which is prone to cracking. The complicated short stub pipes need constant attention to prevent them from binding, which would constrain the necessary expansion and contraction of the annular ring, causing distortion and accelerating cracking.'

What does he like most about the Lysander?

'The Lysander is a very clever aircraft which in many ways tried to do too much and unfortunately came at just the wrong time. The designers researched the Army Cooperation

needs extensively and produced a design that, at its conception, was able to fulfil the intended role and hold its own against the fighters of the time (largely 200mph biplanes). However, the subsequent rapid development of the monoplane fighters with 300mph-plus performance in the immediate lead up to war left it too vulnerable for its intended role in the Western theatre. Had war not intervened I think it would have enjoyed a much longer career as a front-line aircraft, much as its predecessor the Wapiti did.

'Its automatic slat and flap design is a work of aerodynamic art, simple and reliable. It achieves a very useful speed range, a sub-60mph stall and up to 200mph cruise, which, considering its large fixed undercarriage and

ABOVE The complex exhaust system can often affect the serviceability of the Lysander.

being generally a durable and robust design intended for use from rough unprepared strips, is exceptionally good.'

Is there anything that makes his job easier – or more difficult – today than it would have been for the wartime mechanics?

'Due to operational conditions, the mechanics back then would, I suspect, have had worn, damaged and abused aircraft to contend with. They would often have had to work in exposed environments in some pretty inhospitable areas and, with the pressure of war, under severe time constraints. They would have experienced problems with the timely supply of parts and equipment to maintain serviceability.

'However, their aircraft were relatively new, so they would have had full spares, equipment and manufacturers' back-up (if not always when and where they needed it!). In addition, there would have been a large pool of type-specific knowledge that they could have drawn on. This is a situation we can only dream of! For example, the issues we have with the exhaust collector ring only lasting a few years wouldn't have been a problem for them – they would have had an abundant supply or may well have lost the aircraft before it became a problem!

'The biggest hurdle we face in maintaining this aircraft is the lack of spares. Whilst manufacturing spares is nearly always possible, the cost of one-off or small batches is extremely high. This is compounded by the lack of manufacturers' data (drawings etc) and the raw material of the original specifications. Many of the high-quality materials used in aircraft production are no longer made, as there is no modern requirement for them.

'This is further compounded by the regulators requiring a disproportionately high burden of proof (*ie* paperwork) to justify any deviation from the original design. A design deviation includes not only minor changes to the design, manufacturing process or even the surface treatment, but also to any precise material specification changes including those to modern equivalent specifications.

Ground crew at work on a Lysander Mk I (L4712) of No 208 Squadron at RAF Heliopolis, Egypt, in 1939. *(RAF Museum)*

TOP LEFT A wireless operator mechanic tunes a stripped-down radio using a wave-meter.

TOP RIGHT In the pilot's cockpit an instrument mechanic is at work.

CENTRE LEFT Fitters maintain the uncowled Mercury engine.

ABOVE An armourer fits a 0.303in Browning gun into the starboard wheel spat.

LEFT A rigger examines the starboard wing outboard leading edge slat mechanism.

Essentially this means that the cost of the approval paperwork for a newly manufactured part often exceeds the cost of manufacturing the part itself.'

Can you give any recent examples of mechanical problems reported by a Lysander pilot, unexpected or otherwise, that you have had to rectify?

'With a fixed undercarriage, an air-cooled engine, no hydraulics, very simple pneumatics (brakes only), simple electrics and all other systems mechanical, the aircraft is on the whole very reliable. Most issues are found during routine maintenance rather than when the aircraft is in service/on the line. In service there is the occasional mag drop[3] which is often simply an oil-fouled plug. The only other common snag is brake fade which, as previously mentioned, is a design fault coupled with an expectation from today's pilots of much better brake performance! In the '30s most British aircraft still had tail-skids and no brakes. In addition the airports in use at the time were big open grass airfields from which take-offs and landings were made into wind; therefore crosswind landings would have been a rare occurrence.'

Does the need for a current certificate of airworthiness present any particular problems for you or for the inspectors?

'All ex-warbirds and most vintage aircraft operate on a Permit to Fly system, which whilst providing a robust system of airworthiness cannot meet the international requirements necessary for the grant of a full Certificate of Airworthiness. (This is largely to do with spares supply, ongoing type support and the fact that the aircraft design may not meet civil airworthiness standards.) Therefore there are certain restrictions placed on the aircraft, ie it may only fly under day VFR (visual flight rules) conditions, and the carriage of fee-paying passengers is strictly prohibited.

'As mentioned before, the main issue for us is spares supply. This has been greatly

---

[3] In common with all aero piston engines since the First World War there are two independent spark ignition systems for the engine, to provide a redundancy should one fail. These are normally both in operation, but in the pre-flight checks they are tested individually by isolating one system at a time. There is a drop in rpm when operating on just one of the systems: if the drop is excessive then there is a problem with either the spark plug, magneto, ignition harness or associated wiring. This is commonly known as a 'mag drop'.

BELOW The Shuttleworth Lysander nears the end of a long overhaul.

compounded in recent years by regulation, and regulators increasingly applying full burden of Certificate of Airworthiness-style paperwork, auditing and quality requirements on the parts, material, design, manufacture and procurement processes. In the past it was sufficient to apply sound engineering judgement, with the minimum of paperwork to justify the decisions made. To keep them airworthy we can make or have made all the parts required, and in most cases we can and should be able to continue to afford to do so. However, the burden (time and expense) of regulatory compliance remains the most significant threat to the ability to continue to fly the Lysander and her stablemates. However, there are signs that the regulators have accepted the need for a more pragmatic and risk-based approach to this problem. Only time will tell.'

To give an idea of the workload of Jean-Michel and his team, here is an overview of the checks, inspections and servicing that need to be carried out every year on the Lysander (a fuller schedule of tasks is followed every three years, and an even more extensive one for the nine-yearly major overhaul):

Engine
Inspect:
- Cowlings, airscoop, cooling ducts, vents, drains and fasteners.
- Engine bearer – assembly and mountings.
- Engine bulkhead (for damage and sealing).
- Engine installation (for leaks, condition, sealing, mutual interference).
- Crankcase and reduction gear.
- Supercharger/diffuser housing, induction and carburettor.
- Engine and propeller controls, shafts, linkages and cables.
- Starter motor, generator, suppressor and associated wiring.
- Vacuum pump, pipelines, suction relief valve and oil separator.
- Oil and fuel pump, filter housings and pipelines.
- Cylinders, heads, baffles and exhaust system.
- Spark plugs (clean, gap and test).
- HT booster coil, ignition harness, magneto leads and distribution cap (clean if necessary).
- Ki-gas pump, pipelines and unions.

BELOW Technicians busy with maintenance on the Mercury engine.

- Valve gear (charge rockers and adjusting screws with approved grease).
- Service fuel filter.
- Magneto, contact breaker, points, spring, pivot and advance/retard mechanism.
- Air intake and controllable gill spindles.
- Check cylinder compressions by differential method.
- Check drain boost gauge fuel and oil trap.

Propeller

- **Inspect** spinner – check for cracks in the plate around the mounting pedestals.
- **Inspect and lubricate** pitch-change mechanism.
- Check blades all round for condition, damage and corrosion.

Undercarriage

Inspect:

- Wheel fairings, panels, fasteners and associated framework for damage, security and cracking of welds.
- Wheel spokes and spoke attachment to outer rim for cracks.
- Undercarriage main member and attachment to fuselage.

- Wing-strut shackle for cracks.
- Inspect and service tyres and wheels including axles, bearings, slides and runners.
- Inspect and test brake system, pipes, unions and flexible hoses.

Cockpit

Check and lubricate:

- Sliding roof, side panels, shock-absorbing cords and latches, transparencies and supporting structures.
- Pilot's seat, adjusting and damping mechanism.
- Brake operating lever and cable.
- Rudder bar and adjusting device.
- Elevator and rudder control rocker shafts, levers and bearings for cleanliness, wear, security and damage.
- Tailplane adjusting handwheel. Lubricate worm wheel.
- All other controls, levers, switches and cocks for correct operation, locking, leaks etc.

Check:

- Pilot's safety harness, attachment and release mechanism.
- Control column for full free and correct

movement – remove gaiter, check bearings and quadrant pivot/fulcrum bushes for wear, cleanliness and security.

■ Fire extinguisher contents by weight and security of attachment.

■ Instrumentation for legibility, band limit and ranges (where applicable). Readings are consistent with ambient conditions, carbon monoxide detector and lord mounts (engine mounts).

■ Electrical system, instruments, switches, cables and connectors.

■ Placards and markings correct and legible.

■ Compass deviation or steer by card present and legible.

■ Pitot static system for leaks.

Fuselage

Inspect and lubricate:

■ Aileron control: cables at base of quadrant; chains at base of mainplane struts; their connections, pulleys and fairleads.

■ Elevator and rudder control push-pull tubes,

LEFT Controls, linkages and cables inside the cockpit are checked for wear and damage, and free movement.

BELOW The removable panels along the fuselage allow ease of inspection and maintenance.

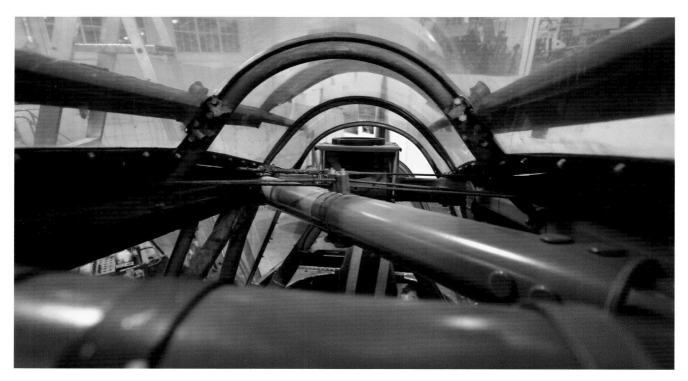

ABOVE Canopy framework, transparencies and supporting structure are inspected.

BELOW This is the supporting structure of the stripped-down tail unit showing tail wheel leg strut and twin ballast weights.

joints, guides/rollers and mountings.
■ Trim control cables, rubbing strips and fairleads.
■ Rear cockpit, transparencies, framework, canopy, slides and latch.

Inspect:
■ Panels, fasteners and supporting framework.
■ Structure, tubes, joints and fishplates.
■ Rear fuselage wooden formers and stringers for damage and security.
■ Rear cockpit seat and harness.

■ Electrical distribution board, cables, connectors and fuses.
■ Battery installation/sealing, cables and terminals.
■ Fuel tank, mounting and pipework.
■ Oil tank, mounting and pipework.
■ Back of instrument panel, tubes, cables etc for condition and chafing.
■ Oil coolers and associated pipework for condition, leaks and security.

Pneumatic system
■ **Inspect** system components, pipework and joints.
■ **Inspect and lubricate** brake relay unit and rudder interconnect tie rod and lever.

Check:
■ Drain – oil and water trap, air filter and compressed air container.
■ Hymatic air compressor, air system oil reservoir and associated pipework.

Tail unit
Inspect:
■ Panels, fasteners and supporting structure.
■ Elevator damping mechanism and stop bracket for wear and security.
■ Elevator and rudder, fabric and drainholes.

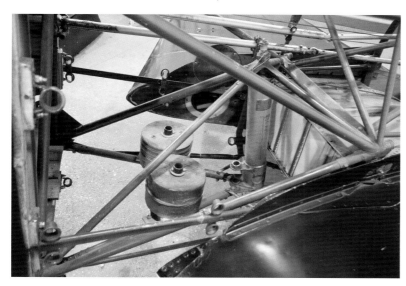

- Ballast weights and mountings.
- Navigation light, cables, terminals and connectors.
- Tail wheel assembly, mounting structure, oleo, friction damper, wheel and tyre.

Inspect and lubricate:
- Fin and tailplane attachments and hinges.
- Rudder and elevator control push-pull tubes, joints, guides, rollers, operating levers and hinges.
- Tailplane adjusting screw jack, trunnion and bottom hinge for wear and security.

Check:
- Elevator spar slides and rubbing strips for excessive wear.
- Trim system, cables, rubbing strips and fairleads.
- Elevator, rudder and tailplane trim. Full and free movement after all panels/fairings refitted.

Mainplanes

Inspect:
- Struts, attachments for security, bowing, corrosion etc and fairings.
- Mainplane, aileron and flap – metal leading edge, fabric covering, drainholes, trailing

ABOVE An unusual view across the top of the mainplanes showing a technician inspecting the starboard wing inboard leading edge slat. Also visible is the rearward sliding Perspex cockpit roof hatch.

edges – for condition, security, damage and signs of deterioration of internal structure.
- Wing root, attachment and supporting structure for condition and security.
- Inner and outer slats for corrosion, deformation, security and for correct seating (ensure not scoring leading edge).
- Navigation light, cables, terminals and connectors.
- Pitot head and drainholes.

Inspect and lubricate:
- Inner slat, flap and flap asymmetric mechanisms, tracks, connecting rods, levers, pivots, cables, pulleys, fairleads, rubbing strips and their attachments as far as possible.
- Outer slat air dampers for security and freedom of movement.
- Aileron and flap hinges and attachment brackets.
- Aileron control system, cables, chains, push rods, quadrants, pulleys, fairleads and their attachments, cable tensions by feel.
- Aileron balance tab and hinge strip for security, cracks and play.

Bibliography and websites

Air Ministry. *Pilot's Notes: Lysander II Aeroplane* (1940 AIR 10/2502).

— *Pilot's Notes: Lysander III and Lysander IIIA Aeroplanes* (1941 AIR 10/2503).

Bertram, Barbara. *French Resistance in Sussex* (Pulborough, Barnworks Publishing, 1995).

Hall, Alan. *Westland Lysander: Warpaint Series No 48* (Luton, Warpaint Books Ltd, 2010).

Hart, Peter. *Somme Success: The Royal Flying Corps and the Battle of the Somme, 1916* (Barnsley, Pen and Sword Books Ltd, 2012).

Kightly, James. *Westland Lysander* (Mushroom Model Publications, 2003).

Mead, Peter. *The Eye in the Air: History of Air Observation and Reconnaissance for the Army, 1785–1945* (London, Her Majesty's Stationery Office, 1983).

Nesbitt-Dufort, Wing Commander John. *Black Lysander* (London, Jarrolds, 1973).

Rémy, Colonel. *Mémoires d'un Agent Secret de la France Libre*, volumes 1–3 (Paris, Éditions France Empire, 1959).

Robertson, Bruce. *Lysander Special* (London, Ian Allan Ltd, 1977).

Verity, Hugh. *We Landed by Moonlight*, revised edition (Manchester, Crécy Publishing Ltd, 1995).

Websites

http://history.whl.co.uk/index.html

http://references.charlyecho.com/?mode=table&dir=/Westland/Lysander

http://www.aviationancestry.com/Aircraft/Westland/Westland-Lysander-1937-1.html

http://www.aviationancestry.com/Aircraft/Westland/Westland-Lysander-1941-6.html

http://www.bharat-rakshak.com/IAF/History/1940s/Lysander.html (Indian Lysanders)

http://www.charles-de-gaulle.org/pages/l-homme/dossiers-thematiques/1940-1944-la-seconde-guerre-mondiale/forces-aeriennes-francaises-libres/analyses/les-avions-fafl.php

http://www.epibreren.com/ww2/raf/2_squadron.html

http://www.eyewitnesstohistory.com/airwar1914.htm

http://www.flightglobal.com/pdfarchive/view/1941/1941%20-%200255.html

http://www.furthermore.org.uk/static/phoenix/penrose/penrose14.htm

http://www.goodall.com.au/warbirds-directory-v6/westland.pdf

http://www.gracesguide.co.uk/James_Bazeley_Petter

http://www.haa-uk.aero/pilots-notes-detail.php?pn-id=9

http://www.pilotfriend.com/photo_albums/timeline/ww2/Westland%20Lysander.htm

http://www.pprune.org/aviation-history-nostalgia/405818-lysander-nickname.html

http://www.raf.mod.uk/rafmarham/aboutus/iiacsqnhistoryww2.cf

http://www.rafjever.org/4squadhistory3.htm http://www.wikipedia.org/

http://www.ww2incolor.com/finnish_forces/Westland+Lysander+I.html

Index